SOMETHING OF OLD SUFFOLK

SOMETHING OF
OLD SUFFOLK

ALLAN JOBSON

ROBERT HALE LIMITED
LONDON

Robert Hale Limited
Clerkenwell House
Clerkenwell Green
London EC1R 0HT

Set in Compugraphic Baskerville by
Ebenezer Baylis & Son Limited,
Worcester, and London
Printed in Great Britain by
Lowe & Brydone Ltd., Norfolk
& bound by Weatherby Woolnough, Northants.

CONTENTS

Spring with its burst is over,
   Summer has had its day,
The scented grasses and clover
   Are cut, and dried into hay;
The singing birds are silent,
And the swallows flown away.

                John Meade Faulkner

ILLUSTRATIONS

Between pages 40 and 41

To Charlotte Anne Jobson.
Born in the jubilee year of Queen Elizabeth II,
the newest of the Jobson line.

FOREWORD

I THINK a period must be placed on the adjectival "old" when writing of a place, a building or a person, otherwise there is no limit to its extent. In this case it refers to the years of Queen Victoria and those prior to the First World War, which more or less compass an era.

Thus it brings to mind the countryside before the internal combustion engine changed the whole world, when fragrance filled the air; that was also filled with light and purity. It was a scene that Thomas Churchyard had painted, Henry Bright and the Smythe brothers, which had lasted until I was a child old enough to remember. When country lanes like those of Hogweed, Maybush, and Honey Pot meant what they said. And when the menfolk and the womenfolk belonged, by reason of long tenure. They were individuals every one as they look out from an old photograph, such as Billy Besant, wearing a moleskin "whiskit" and a French hat, "shummaker" and Parish Clerk at Darsham "chuurch"; as his father before him.

It is of them I think when I write of old Suffolk—that wonderful race skilled in all the arts of making ends meet, even to doing a bit of physicking—over which time has cast a charm. The Sutton Hoo treasure and the gold torques that lie under the Suffolk soil are too far away in time. My thoughts go to the dear old folk I knew who now lie under the churchyard soil, whose names are fragrant, as were their homespun clothes, and their pantries also.

One of the chief pleasures of a spring or summer afternoon, after Charlie Chambers had dropped his penny into the collecting shoe at the chapel of my mother's village of Middleton, was a walk home with a friend, along the scented way to the Moor, or Valley Farm, or even as far as the Yew Tree. Perhaps Mahalah would walk home with grandmother, or Naomi with Cousin Rodwell. Neither would the conversation necessarily be about the sermon, or the ability, or lack of it, of the preacher, or if any one of them was going to brew this week. Rhoda at the shop was inclined to keep to herself, but if anyone cared to call in they were welcome. Folks used to say whether you went to hers on a Sunday or a Monday the house was as clean as a new pin. As for the menfolk, they also paired off, but their conversation was about pigs and stock, and how that ten acre was a-hickling along to a remarkable degree.

Not even fashion worried the women with their bonnets and shawls. Because it was not something new that caused a flutter of envy in the ranks, but something old that had stood the test of years. After all, old Aunt Rebecca was rarely put out when she burnt a hole in her bombazine dress which she had had since she married. 'That dutty owd muck regular flew out o' the fire like an evil spirit, afore I could help meself!' Mrs Marjoram prided herself that her dress had belonged to her mother — that was a rum time ago — but complained that when her mother had it new it was black, now it had turned a bit green. But, there, things will wear out!

They were not all saints, though there was, and is, an area in Suffolk, called "The Saints", but that refers to the churches. The non-saints were to be found amongst the smugglers, the poachers; and, I fear, amongst the old horse-dealers. But we must let them lie, side by side, in that same churchyard, with spleenwort or hart's-tongue as a memorial.

And there were brave men for there were none to equal the lifeboatmen. That old Suffolk coast-line was often terrible in the days of sail, but the heroism was there under the sou'westers. And if you want visible evidence go into the Aldeburgh churchyard and you will find it.

That old Suffolk was almost intact until the railways came. True, there were roads that went all the way to London, along which the coaches and the waggons trundled. But you did not go in those unless you were forced. And there were the old Hoys that went from Slaughden Quay, such as the William and George, Amity, Plough, John and Jane, Heart of Oak, Harriet, even a Friends of Eliza. To be tied up at Harrison's Wharf, St Katherine's near the Tower; Fenning's Wharf, New London Bridge; Galley Wharf, Lower Thames Street; Custom House and Wool Quays.

The railways were quite different and my grandmother was amongst the first generation of those who saw their gals dispersed into the great Wen. I think she must have had a slight palpitation when she said goodbye. Because as far as her early years were concerned she had only moved from Yoxford to Middleton, and you could do that on foot, or pony cart. I think it wanted a bit of courage in both mother and daughter; as for grandfather, he shed a few tears, and went a bit husky.

And thereby grew the memories, such as the one I received from a well travelled man in South Africa: 'Dear old Suffolk, I would love to see it again, but I know my Eyke primrose wood was swept away to make room for an aerodrome. Do the bluebells still grow in Martlesham woods?

'There was a dear old character, Miss Harriet Churchyard, who used to preside in the Seckford Library. Clad in white shawl and lace cap, inscribing the name of each book and borrower in a large book with a quill pen — Victoriana personified.'

He goes on to tell of a Suffolk ·character in Woodbridge: 'Old Honky, we never knew him by any other name. He used to pull a hand-barrow laden with sacks of coke from the gas works, and as he came round the corner bent double between the shafts, he gave out a large "Honk". His allegiance on Saturday was to the Salvation Army on the Market Hill, but on

Sunday he blew the organ at the Wesleyan Chapel.'

Another writes from near home, where her grandfather, as sexton, found the Wenhaston Doom. 'I have known the thrill of a ride on the Southwold Railway, daily for four years to Southwold.

'Also, as a girl, for our Sunday School treat we went in decorated waggons to Dunwich, and I remember Watling's tea shed facing the sea, also a lifeboat shed, where tables were laid out for our lunch and tea. And on the right of the lane facing the sea on the corner, was a small sweet shop and fancy goods kept by Mrs Brown, my mother's aunt (she was also related to my grandmother). Also my grandparents had a farm at Dingle and were brought away on horseback once or twice by Mr Grimsey of St Helena farm, when high seas threatened the farm.'

'Referring to those huge coppers. I came down the back stairs one evening about eleven p.m. and found my brother-in-law having a bath in one of them. His head was just peeping out, as he sat in it.'

'I am a Londoner but my father was a Suffolk man. I was interested in how they kept warm in those days. Their boots would be made of stout, stubborn leather and damp and cold from working on the land. My dad said they warmed them by putting a hot cinder in them and rolling it about before putting them on. Sometimes it would get wedged in the toe and they would have to hit it with a poker and crush the cinder and then shake it out. His father was a Prim [Methodist] and had to walk four miles to a cottage meeting and six miles to a chapel and was always being threatened with being turned off the place for being a chapel man. But they were very good to him at the end. Gave him a pension and a cottage. When he got beyond walking to chapel my father used to push him there in a wheelbarrow.

'My father spoke of the pranks they cut at Harvest Home.

One man stood on his head on the top of the last load and the waggon gave a jolt and threw him off and broke his neck.

'My father went to Barnham Chapel. There was a story as to how it came to be built. The people prayed for a new chapel but they couldn't get permission from the Duke of Grafton. He died suddenly and the idea got about that the Prims had prayed the Duke to death. The Prims said no. They prayed for every obstacle to be removed. The Duke being a bachelor his brother succeeded him and the Prims waited on him for their chapel.

'He said to them "I know what is being said about the death of my brother. I never expected to reach this position and I wish to keep it as long as I can. You can have your chapel and I will give you £5 a year if at every service you will pray for a long life for the Duke of Grafton." Their prayers must have been very effectual for the Duke lived to be ninety-five. The chapel in question was built in 1865.'

How to make scraps: 'The surplus fat from the back of a pig when it is being cut into joints is boiled after being cut into small pieces and the fat liquid is put into pans and is eventually lard. When all the fat has been extracted it leaves what we call "scraps". My mother used to make scrap short-cakes which were very tasty.'

'My mother's brother had a farm between Dovercourt and Harwich and there I spent many holidays in childhood. I can remember getting up very early and riding horseback to a distant part of the farm. It was no hardship to walk back to breakfast.

'How we loved the old brick floors, the real *copper* copper where my aunt brewed the beer and the huge brick copper where the grain was kept for the poultry. Even at twelve years of age I could not see inside and my uncle said that three people could stand in it.'

This place was virtually destroyed in the 1914 war by being made into a fortress; and it was never the same again. Then the letter turns to Suffolk.

'Would you believe that I have bought herrings on Dunwich beach from Chris Watling for twenty-four a shilling? And they were delicious.'

'Reference to grandfather's tallow plaster. Many a one have I had as a child. Also a specific such as a grey powder (ugh!) and arnica and senna, which still have a place in my medicine cupboard.'

'My grandparents were wonderful people and I had a wonderful childhood, although we were very poor, for my grandad was an invalid for seventeen years before he died. Gran who was a Barker before marriage used to say of the Noys, "Oh, they are the two Ps, poor and proud". I too am proud to come from such a strain.'

'I would also mention that my father attended a dame school, at a small house in Wherstead Road, Ipswich, where he paid one penny a week, and as they took their places every morning they had to sing:

> We go to our places with clean hands and faces,
> And pay great attention to all we are told,
> Or else we shall never be happy as ever,
> For early is better than silver and gold.'

A letter from Louisana ends: 'America is a great country, everything modern, but dear Suffolk has something I have never found here.'

'My mother was born in Aldeburgh and my grandfather had the cobbler's shop there. I spent many happy days round and about the haunts of Aldeburgh, Leiston, Theberton, and Saxmindham.'

'I was born 5th July 1905 in the policeman's cottage at

Theberton where my parents on coming to Theberton stayed for a few months till the teacher's house was ready. I went to the village school, Framlingham College and finally, at enormous expense to the R.M.A. Woolwich from which I was commissioned into the Gunners.

'Conditions in those days sound incredible now, water from the well, outside lavatory, oil lamps, candles. We used to have a maid from the village who brushed my sister's hair before we went to bed; she used to tell us ghost stories — after which we crept to bed with our candles. Saturday morning baking, Sunday, Church, Sunday School and reading (no games). My father was the churchwarden.

'My father took standards four to six, and my mother one to three in the village school — all in the same room. There was one other uncertificated teacher who had the infants who were separated by a partition. Some of the children (from the Sluice) walked three miles there and three miles back to school each day.

'A Miss Doughty took me at Sunday School, and Mr Isaacson was the clergyman whom we loved.'

'I am a great grandson of an Edward Barham, farmer, born at Badingham Suffolk, in 1798. He migrated to Tillington in Sussex in the late 1820s, and the farm he tenanted is still being run by two of his grandsons, now well in their seventies [1959]. One of his sons, Edward, went to Suffolk for his bride, marrying his second cousin Ellen Barham of, I think, Shelly House, Bruisyard, her mother being a Shelly from Badingham.

'Great grandfather Edward was, I gather, the result of a runaway match, his mother being formerly a Miss Thurlow of Saxmundham.

'Great Aunt Ellen, whom I knew very well, died in the 1930s, in her ninetieth year and spoke broad Suffolk all her life. Her brother William lived at Bruisyard Hall and farmed about 400 acres as a tenant of the Earl of Stradbroke.

'I knew, or have known, four generations of Barhams and in the main they are so much the kind of people you describe that I feel they are of the same stock.'

'My owd Aunt in Fressingfield lives at the foot of Harleston Hill, you can't miss it, the owd bec still runs aside the garden [1950], something they can't easily take away and where bullaces still grow, bore for me to have a feed. The old lady said I deserved to have the belly ache—or perhaps not so polite.'

As someone has said, it is in trivia that the poignancy of life lies.

1

A SUFFOLK VILLAGE ECONOMY

Let not ambition mock their useful toil,
Their homely joys, and destiny obscure;
Nor grandeur hear with a disdainful smile,
The short and simple annals of the poor.

Have you ever wondered where those old compilers of directories got their information? Suffolk seems to have had at least
three in the nineteenth century. If you study their work you
will gather a very concise history of the county. After all you
do not want to know who Monulf was in King Edward's time,
or about Alveva a free woman, or Aluric a freeman; but you
might like to meet Philemon Backhouse, a farmer in 1855, or
Kezia Hunt who farmed in 1844; the village in question being
Middleton-cum-Fordley in the Blything Hundred of East Suffolk.

If you take the first of the directories done by Mr John Kirby
of Wickham Market, 'who took an actual survey of the whole
county in the years 1732–4', you will find an account of its
'Situation, extent, towns, roads, Members of Parliament,
valuations of each parish, patrons of ditto, High Sheriffs, a list
of Fairs, rivers, minerals, curiositys, antiquities, biography'.
But you will not find any reference to a Noah Foulsham, or
even a Lucy Richbell who followed her father (or could it have
been her husband?) in 1855 as a farmer. It was left to William
White to do that.

I think William was a wonderful man because he not only
accomplished a *History, Gazeteer and Directory of Suffolk,*

but 'similar works for Norfolk, Lincolnshire, Yorkshire and many other counties'. These included 'Histories, & Statistics & Topographical Descriptions of all the Hundreds, Liberties, Unions, Boroughs, Towns, Ports, Townships, Villages and Hamlets, including Seats of Nobility and Gentry'. What more could one want under the hand of one man? All done from Sheffield of all places.

Presumably Walter White who wrote *Eastern England from the Thames to the Humber* in 1865 was his son. He was certainly a good companion and noticed all kinds of tit-bits about life in general, such as the women in Essex who used to congregate about a certain inn known as the "Royal Oak" and drink themselves to sleep: '"I tell ye I didn't," exclaimed a lady as I passed. "I tell ye I didn't, 'twas Mrs Jackson as emptied the bottle. She can take a drop o' gin, she can, comfortabler than any women I ever see".'

Returning to William, it is true he lists the tradesmen, the farmers, occasional gentlemen and the parsons, but not the majority of the folk who made up the inhabitants; the poor old labouring class. Who provided him with the lists? it must have been the overseers who levied the poor rates. He certainly gives Middleton a good start, describing it as a well built village.

Middleton also possessed a wonderful overseer in a William Free who kept the book from 1808 to 1821. He came of a family who had been there for 300 years or more, and whose family yet remains. These were written up by a delightful old man, Israel Nichols, whom I knew, obviously with a view to publication, but which never saw the light of day. The entries begin in 1750, running on to 1838, and give an account of village life.

First we are told about the two churches in the one churchyard and the animosity between the parsons. This was settled by the Solomon-like judgement of the Bishop of Norwich in 1620 who placed the two hamlets under one incumbent, who officiated in each alternately. We are then told of the Middleton Poors' Estate which was of such antiquity that no one knew from whence it came. It consisted of eleven small ground-rents and town houses standing in The Street, where they presumably still exist.

In 1750 a Widow Dove appears on the scene who received aid at 2s. per week, but the next year someone was paid 2s. for laying out the body of the poor old soul; and her coffin cost 8s. At this time the name of Newson is recorded, a good old Suffolk name of some antiquity, which still survives; also that of J. Fryer. In addition to the weekly allowances one person was given 3½ yards of cloth costing 3s., a pair of shoes, 3s., half a pint of wine and a handkerchief, 6d. I suppose the latter was a piece of turkey twill for the neck; and turf was distributed for firing, otherwise known as flags. These disbursements were signed under the name of Sam Crowe for 1750 and John Preeves 1751, when a Mrs Towler was given a bottle of wine. I wonder if this was Communion wine in one of those funny old bottles; and as there were no sticky labels at that time it would have had one tied on the neck like a medicine bottle. It is to be hoped that Mrs Towler enjoyed it to the last drop. A Dr Bloomfield was paid £2.12s.6d. for medical attention to all the poor, which was a lot of money. I expect the vet would have done as well.

John Last, another good old Suffolk name appears as the next overseer. He removed a Widow Scarlett for 3s. But as it does not say the destination, it must have been to the workhouse which was at Saxmundham. He also splashed out 5s. for daubing (plastering) of the Town House.

William Calver comes next but he had to spend 50s. for repairing this same old dwelling. He seems to have been followed by John Stanford in 1753. He buried J. Pyrer for 21s.6d., had three chimneys swept for 1s. and credited the parish with £1.4s.2d. received from John Courtnall 'for his house standing on the Green', which was due at Easter 1753. This is the first reference to the ground rents.

The 30th May, 1753, is the date of an agreement drawn up by Joseph Gooda and John Lay, overseers, 'to attend all the poor of the parish that are chargeable to them or shall become so for three years from Easter last, and find them all necessary physick and surgery to the best of my judgement, and to be allowed ten shillings and sixpence for every fracture and to have it paid to me or my heirs every Easter, as witness my hand Wm Gibbon. Witnessed by Jno Preeves, John Willson.'

In 1754 Ann Dove, daughter or sister of the widow, cost the overseers 48*s*. for smallpox. The next year they paid 9*s*. for a coat, 1*s*. for a neck of veal and 9*d*. for a shift and a sheet. 1755 Philip Wade took over, he allowed Widow Moore 3*s*. weekly, while others received only 6*d*. It is too late now to ask why this great disparity. He also paid Thomas Gilbert's rates of 12*s*. and the remaining part of Mary Studd's charges 'not allowed by the man', 2*s*.6*d*., and a further 8*s*. 'more than the fellow allowed'. This is a reference to bastardy and other orders that the overseers very conveniently made up what others neglected to pay, and so kept the peace.

1757, with John Stanford as overseer, saw heavy expenditure owing to an epidemic of smallpox. He had to pay a bill of £7.7*s*.9½*d*. for that, 3*s*. for ringing the bell and digging a grave. The Kelsale sexton also received 3*s*. for a burial and Mr Bence the minister 1*s*. In consequence the Poor Rate rose from 6*d*. to 1*s*.6*d*.

In 1758 Sam Whiting paid £6.1*s*.0*d*. for repairing the bridge, 1*s*.6*d*. for making a gown for a widow and 1*s*. for mending her shoes. It is to be hoped they did not pinch.

In 1760 Richard Savage relieved in twenty-six weeks nineteen families at a cost of £19.4*s*.0*d*., and two widows were laid forth 10*s*. He also paid 3*s*.6*d*. for breeches and 10*s*. for two coffins. But it was not all paying out because he sold the goods of the widow, presumably deceased, for 30*s*.6*d*., with which he credited the parish, and ended up with a credit balance of 1*s*.9¾*d*. So he might have been a Victorian draper. (This same year comes the curious statement that Sam Crowe lost 5*s*. on Fordley Rectory, which looks like a wager.)

1761 brought in John Thrower who introduced the first

reference to coal, when he gave away £1.0s.6d. worth. He also paid 5d. for a letter, which our guide says is the first reference to a letter, and made an agreement with Doctor Garner of Yoxford at £4 a year to look after the sick for seven years.

In 1767 Robert Foulsham was overseer and the House of Industry at Bulcamp comes into the news. Suffolk was one of the first counties to build these institutions and Bulcamp was opened in October 1765 with fifty-six inmates, to be the dread and fear of all the surrounding poor for many a long year. He paid to the poor that went to Bulcamp 6s., expenses 4s., 'my journey 1s.'. There had been a determined effort to destroy the House as soon as it was built. Foulsham adds, 'the accounts are alright tho' they are a jumble'.

In 1786 Simon Butcher was overseer. He stated, country fashion: 'On balancing ye Town meeting ye book was 5¾d. in debt', and added rather enigmatically, 'six shillings was then added which I never received'. This was the time when large numbers of children were sent to the cotton factories of Lancashire, to work like little slaves; but Middleton decided otherwise to its eternal honour. The overseers even bought a little book on the subject by a Robert Blinco, costing 5s. He had been one of these sad little apprentices.

In 1789 Mr Packard's barn was burnt. This was evidently the tithe barn because Mr Packard was the rector. (Could it have been arson?) In 1795 the following signed at the vestry meeting that the accounts were in order: D. Packard, Sam. Wilson, Richard Savage, Wm Nunn, N. Wilson, Jno Bedwell, Simon Butcher, Robert Mashling and Jos. Balls. The accounts for 1800 show a bill for a coal house £1.10s.

The coal was brought from Aldeburgh, where it was unloaded from the Billyboy ketches and sold by the chaldron of 36 bushels.

1806 saw the start of payment of the overseers of one guinea a quarter. The justices in 1801 were D. E. Davey and Charles Blois, both of Yoxford. In 1810 comes the rather strange entry: 'Paid Leiston Overseers, Middleton's part of the bill of maintenance of Button's Substitute's wife and two children £2.6s.8d.' (This is a reference to the Militia when eligible men could obtain a substitute for serving during the threat of the Napoleonic wars.)

1810–11 paid Turner for setting out the bounds between Theberton and Middleton, and I. Savage for going with him 3s. Then comes the outburst: 'Paid the Clerk [of Court] for examining these accounts *which they never see, heard or know anything about*, 4s. 1811, Census warden and self, taking an account of the Inhabitants and journey to Yoxford 10s.' 1813 saw them taking a woman to Wenhaston because that was her settlement, but a little later she was back again and arrested. Then in 1815 comes the first entry of tolling the Harvest Bell, 6s.8d., which seems a lot of money. Presumably this was the Gleaning Bell. But in 1816 comes this: 'Going round the Town [village] to provide work for labourers on reduced terms 5s.' and further, '. . . writing to other parishes on account of their poor and other such writing etc. occasioned by these particular times'.

These "particular times" were the worst ever experienced in rural England. The Government had started a scheme under which the unemployed were given so much a week, it being arranged that each farmer in the village in turn should employ these men on certain days at reduced pay. The men were known as roundsmen.

In 1821 William Free obtained the following receipt from his successor: 'I, John Johnson, do hereby acknowledge to have received of Wm Free, the now present overseer, one shilling and one penny farthing, the above named Town stock, having been laid out according to the order and satisfaction of the inhabitants of the Parish, 7 April 1821.'

It appears that Free loved to have everything in order; he was a neat writer and once started to make an index but only reached two letters when he gave up in despair. He was not the first to start such a thing but holds the record for making the shortest one.

Free's work is shown in the particulars given of the second census of 1811 and also that of 1821. 1811 gives inhabited houses seventy-seven, occupied by 121 families; uninhabited one. Persons engaged in trade thirty-nine, in agriculture seventy-nine, in neither five. Males 274, females 290; total 564. No houses building. Taken by Noah Foulsham and W. Free.

1821, Inhabited houses, Fordley fifty-two. Families eighty-one, none building, all inhabited.

Inhabited houses, Middleton twenty-six. Families forty-eight, none building, all inhabited. Engaged in agriculture, Fordley fifty-five. Chiefly in trade seventeen. In neither nine. Engaged in agriculture, Middleton twenty-two. Chiefly in trade eighteen. In neither eight. Males, Fordley 170, females 181: total 351. Males, Middleton 109, females 104: total 213. Grand total 564. In the united parishes there were fifteen persons between seventy and eighty years of age; four persons between eighty and ninety, and one person between ninety and 100. One wonders how 121 families got into seventy-seven houses in 1811, and 129 into seventy-eight in 1821. In my mother's day, thirty to forty years on, space was rather cramped for a single family in one house.

In 1829 comes the curious passage, 'Mould of Green, sold and credited to the parish, £1.19s.0d.'. Then in 1831 a Parish Constable's staff was purchased for 5s., evidently because of threatened riots. 1832 brings the entry: 'Making Juror's List and Clerk 8s., fifteen people registered 15s.', which was the first reference to a Voters' List. Also this same year comes the first reference about schools.

The 1835 audit was not allowed and that for 1836 was not much better when Richard Garrett's bill for a weighing machine (for corn?) costing £2.5s.6d. was disallowed; and the cost of carting it was also scratched. But this year gives the first reference to a postman; and 1837, when the rector signed the book, was the first time he was noted as such. Also the trustees of the Wesleyan Chapel paid 6s.8d. for their ground rent.

This overseers' account book ends with an appreciation of William Free, who was overseer and schoolmaster. I wonder where he kept his little school? Presumably in his own cottage which may have been a town house on the Green. He was born in 1758 and served with tact and judgement during England's worst period of agricultural depression. He not only entered his own items clearly, but retraced the earlier accounts and added interesting items about the parish that had not been recorded. To do this he turned the book end to end and utilized the blank spaces. He even noticed that a rate of 4*d*. in the pound was 6*d*. short and duly remarked the mistake. A clock to his memory was placed in the church tower on 22nd February 1939 by the will of his great grandson, the Reverend Richard William Free, vicar of St Clement's, Fulham.

We might now turn to William White's *Directory* of 1844, when my grandfather was a young man and knew everyone of the names given. There were nineteen farmers and their fields were criss-crossed by paths leading to their dairy doors. There were two tailors and no less than four boot and shoe makers, one of whom is described as a shop keeper. Jacob Barnes kept a beerhouse and Robert Foulsham the "Bell", and was also a wheelwright. Henry and Augustus Richbell were malsters, William Allen was a fishmonger and William Noller the butcher. Samuel Hunt was a grocer and draper, William Ludbrook a shopkeeper, and there were two joiners. John Brown was a bricklayer and also my grandmother's brother. He left a lot of memorials behind when he moved into the churchyard under a brick-built tomb, chiefly pebble-fronted cottages such as those still in use in Mill Street. William Bedwell was a blacksmith, Thomas Geater a farmer and corn miller and Kezia Hunt was also a farmer.

John Davey was credited with being a schoolmaster, although I think it was Mrs Davey who kept the school to which my mother and aunt went. John was a mere snuff taker. Joseph Broom must have been in his youth because he is described as a hawker. The population was then 599, and I wonder how all those shopkeepers and tradesmen got their livelihood when pockets were so empty. However, a William Free went to Ipswich every Tuesday and Friday.

We might now turn to the 1879 *Directory* of Mr Kelly, when we shall find the picture altered but slightly. For instance a Church School was built in 1850 by the Reverend Edmund Hollond at a cost of £400 and Ann Arnold was the schoolmistress in 1855. I wonder if she was the first; she may well have been of the same family as the famous Master of Rugby. But now William Spall and his sister or daughter, Miss Eliza Spall had taken over. Mr Joseph Broom had grown into a shopkeeper, with a post office; and had also become an institution. Matthias Wright kept the "Bell" and was also a farmer; but there is no mention of a beerhouse.

There were still seventeen farmers and one man bearing the delightful name of Philemon Backhouse was at the Garden House farm, so he must have linked sweetness to that other vegetation that is the staff of life. There were only three shoemakers, to wit George Baldry, William Richard Rouse, and John Newson who was also the parish clerk. Robert Foulsham was still the wheelwright but had moved away from the "Bell", Samuel Martin Spall had now taken over as blacksmith and Isaac Laughlin was the miller. But the tailors had shut up shop and moved on, and Robert Barnes was the only foil to Joseph Broom. Joseph Fisk was the builder and there were no less than four carpenters, John Larter, Henry Matkin, Samuel Mayhew, Jessie Merrels.

John Davey still had an academy although there was the Church School. It was wonder what they could do for a copper or two in the way of a bit o' larnin. Perhaps it was not so much the amount of learning that was imparted as the interest in acquiring more.

Now appears on the scene names of my mother's family which had populated the village since the eighteenth century. Francis Barham is described as a market gardener and Joseph Barham as a gardener. That name was to be associated with

the parish until the middle of the next century until it completely died out. John Newson was the parish clerk, the ground
rents were the same at £3.9s.0d., and the population in 1871
was 526. The delivery of letters commenced at 7.30 a.m.

Middleton is described as being on the banks of the Minsmere, a little stream that meanders along green meadows
made green by its waters. It seems to come from nowhere, but
its destination is certain, made by Dutchmen, through a brick-
built sluice, and thus to the sea. In my grandfather's time and
long years before, it was noted for eels, babbed by boys who
could be seen at evening with long home-made fishing rods,
making their way to where such delicacies could be found.

The village itself is most pleasantly undulating, with gentle
curves that hide the church, although that stands on a bit of a
rise. The old manor house stands on the slope of one of those
gentle hills, and Hill Farm by its very name on another. But
you catch the note of its contours by such names as Valley
Farm and Vale Farm, and of its flatness by Fen Street Farm.
The little stream runs along its north side veering to the east;
and of course there are a lot of ditches on the banks of which
the paigles grow, the meadow sweet and the forget-me-not.
Also by that stream grow the alders, mostly pollarded, that
provide the wistfulness of soft green under a wide blue sky
where a lizard or two peeps in and out. It seems hardly possible
that such a small burble of water could sustain a Water Mill
Farm, but so it was. It is still there in name if not in nature.

There are also the great trees, the oaks that once made Suffolk famous, the elms with their individuality of shape,
beeches with their own peculiar beauty; and an occasional
aspen that for ever sings a muted song. There was one beside
the pond at Rackford Farm. A pond that never dried up but
which no one thought to get lyrical about when the
homecomers took their little draught.

> Four ducks on a pond,
> A grass bank beyond,
> A blue sky of spring,

White clouds on the wing;
What a little thing
To remember for years —
To remember with tears!
William Allingham

Of course, like every other village, Middleton was divided into one or two manors; in fact there were three. There was Middleton Chickering, Manor of Brent Fen and Middleton Austins. A Court book of the latter for 1694–1754 came to light in the early part of the twentieth century, containing information of no less than sixty-six courts. Amongst other things it discloses that this village had its own individuality, because the custom of Borough English obtained there. In the proceedings of a General Court Baron held the twelfth day of April, 1736, before Thomas Mulliner, Gent., Steward, there, it is recorded that the youngest son of any tenant of this Manor is Heir-at-Law.

Amongst the *obits* and admissions are several interesting names, such as Agnes Pulham, widow, May 1698. John ffoulsham February 1704. Thomas Pulham, March 1718, Gent. Margaret Pulham, August 1740, with another John ffoulsham, March 1744, and Robert Drane Gent., December 1752. Thus showing at least two gentlemen but no yeomen. It is given to the Admissions to to provide the latter, such as Thomas Eade, yeoman, September 1695, John ffoulsham, June 1701, James Brain, February 1704, John Newson, farmer, Robert Catchpole, Henry Barrow and Thomas Pulham of Austins, Gent., June 1717. This distinction between yeomen and gentlemen had led to a correspondence in the *East Anglian Notes and Queries* for 1899–1900, because of a brass in Middleton Church with this inscription:

Here lieth the body of Anthony Pettow
Yeoman who married Frauncis Daughter of
Thomas Bishope of Kelleshall Yeoman wch
Caused this marble stone to be layd who

Departed this life the XVjth of November
Anno Dni 1610 of the age of Liiij

Above the lettering is his full-length portrait. He has
moustache and beard and wears his hair cut short. Round his
neck is a ruff. He has a close-fitting tunic buttoned from the
neck to waist, with two buttons at each wrist. A narrow belt
round the waist is fastened in front with hook and eye. His
breeches are full but tighten towards the knees, where they fit
quite closely. He wears stockings and shoes with laces tied in a
bow. Over his shoulders hangs a cloak, which comes down to
just below the knees. It has a collar, and is unfastened at the
neck. The arms from the elbows appear from beneath his
cloak and his hands are clasped in prayer. A man of the
yeoman rank was seldom buried *inside* the church, and
perhaps still more seldom commemmorated with a brass.

Alas, I fear he was swept away when the thatch caught fire
and the dear old church was all but destroyed.

In a ten-generation pedigree, quoted by Charles Partridge,
himself of a yeoman family, the same person was sometimes
styled gentleman, sometimes yeoman, sometimes farmer, but
could only be termed gentleman if he bore arms. Partridge
then proceeds to quote Jane Austen's *Emma*:

Emma is speaking of Robert Martin, whom Mr Knightly
calls (in Chapter VIII) a gentleman-farmer, and says '"A
young farmer . . . is the very last sort of person to raise my
curiosity. The yeomanry are precisely the order of people with
whom I feel I can have nothing to do. A degree or two lower,
and a creditable appearance might interest me; I might hope
to be useful to their families in some other way or other. And a
farmer can need none of my help, and is, therefore, in one
sense, as much above my notice as in every way he is below it."'
(Chapter IV).

2

MIDDLETON BELL

Souls of poets dead and gone,
What Elysium have ye known,
Happy field or mossy cavern,
Choicer than the Mermaid Tavern?
Have ye tippled drink more fine
Than mine host's Canary wine?
                              Keats

According to the 1879 Kelly's *Directory* there were a large
number of "Bell Inns" in Suffolk, thirty-two to be exact,
followed by six "Five Bells", eleven "Six Bells", three "Eight
Bells" and two "Ten Bells"; the latter at Stonham Parva and
Bury St Edmunds. I notice that someone has written to the effect that not all these are named after the rings in the neighbouring church steeple but rather are after handbell ringers. I
like to think that the steeple claims the relationship. It was so
at Stonham Parva, where an enthusiastic incumbent managed
to install ten bells in his belfry, of which he was commendably
proud.

There was also a "Black Bell" in Museum Street, Ipswich,
which may have had connection with a firm of bell-founders.
Or it might have had a more sinister side as related to public
hangings.

As far as Middleton and its surroundings were concerned,
there was a "Bell" at Saxmundham, but that was on an important route, no less than the London-Yarmouth Road, and
was described as a 'Family and Commercial Hotel and Posting

House'. But a far greater rival was the "Eight Bells" at Kelsale, just over the hill from Middleton, the belfry of which gave out a really beautiful sound to match the steeple that had a coronal at the top that gave it a lace-like effect.

I wonder if once upon a time the beer brewed and sold at the Middleton "Bell" was the charge of the monks from Ranulph de Glanville's Leiston Abbey, when the local churches were in their patrimony?

Middleton "Bell" has been always rather retiring, tucked away in a corner, but it is within sight and sound of the five bells in the belfry of the old church of the Holy Trinity, which manages to sit on the only bit of rising ground in the heart of the village. I do not know of anything more lovely than on a summer's morning, when the corn was studded with scarlet to walk along that so peaceful village street, past the old rectory and the new, to the ting-tang of those delightful bells that had such a Flemish flavour. I can hear them yet, although they have long ceased to greet the morning of a new day.

Like the church, Middleton "Bell" was thatched and before Queen Victoria had achieved her jubilee, it was kept by a Matthias Wright, who was also a farmer. I would hazard a guess that he brewed his own beer. If not perhaps his wife did, as it often seemed a woman's job. Although the man got the things ready such as cleaning out the casks and getting up the water, a woman had that sense of just when to do this or that, as in baking in the old brick ovens. I wonder if her name was Nancy? If so perhaps it was she who said: 'I 'ont be called Nancy! Thass the name of an owd cow.' Certainly the ringers must have known of the quality of the beer because ringing always seemed to be a thirsty job. And, let it be noted, they seldom stopped for the "sarvice", or took a place in the choir. But they might have been found in the "Bell".

In the years of long ago there were no less than three inns in Middleton. The "Old Plough" stood at the top of the hill as one goes to Theberton from what was known as Middleton Corner. And the "King's Head", which one I do not know, at

Garden House corner. It may well have been that of St Edmund, King and Martyr, or even Charles I. But the "Bell" has been always the most important, small as it is, because it has been in the middle of the houses, and more than probably was the venue for certain parish meetings; and it was not unknown to smuggling since it is so close to the marshes.

In 1844 it was held by George Mills, but that was when the Reverend Joseph White was curate, who built the new rectory and planted a magnificent magnolia before the front door. And Queen Victoria was happy with her Consort and young family.

On 11th September 1837, when that same queen was but newly come to the throne, having been eyed by her cousin George, a meeting was held at the "Bell" by the principal landowners of the period. They came to enquire into the parish boundaries, because an application about these had been made by the Tithe Commissioners; and one of them, a Mr Meerest was appointed to fix the boundaries. It took him to the next March to complete the task, marking the names of the fields on the map, fields which my grandfather knew so well. Such as Old four Acres, Little two Acres, Great nine Acres, Walnut Tree Hill, Sugar Pightle, Mardle Meadow (reminiscent of the time when they had a little chat together); not forgetting Devil's Pit (which I think I can remember, but since has been filled in as a refuse dump; and Rawbones and Waste which seem to have been a sand pit.

Which reminds me that a relation of mine by marriage had been cycling about and when he came home he was telling my old aunt where he had been; she exclaimed 'that was Devil's Lane'! 'Oh,' said he quite innocently, "I didn't know who it belonged to!'

Near the corner devoted to brewing, stood the village pump, which must have been very handy for all concerned, including the "Bell" itself; the most neighbourly thing in any settlement. The houses nearby were wholly lucky because all they had to do was to pop out and get a pailful as and when required; others had to walk long distances. Somehow or other that old pump got into private ownership and there was a regular rumpus. But the trouble was solved by a lorry driver who demolished it.

Broom's shop was rather too near the "Bell" corner, because two of his sons, Azor and Alma found it a great attraction. I think it led them into the churchyard sooner than they would have gone naturally.

One thing more: the "Bell" yard was used by a travelling photographer and my old aunt, my mother's younger sister, when she was a little girl of five years old, wearing a nice little print frock, hair parted in the middle, seated on a Suffolk chair, with small button boots and holding an orange, had her picture taken on glass. I have it still and have never ceased to realize what a nice little thing she was and what a kind old lady she became.

I expect she grew up under the influence of Dr Watts:

> Though I am now in younger days
> Nor can tell what will befall me,
> I'll prepare for ev'ry place,
> Where my growing age shall call me.

3

DUFFERS MEADOWS

Of alle the floures in the mede,
That love I most these floures whyte and rede,
Swiche as men callen daysies in our toun.
Chaucer

Someone writing from Norfolk said they always thought Suffolk people silly. Well they might if they did not understand and know what lay behind the old vocabulary. For example, it was reasonable to think thus of a village that had a tract of ground which they called Duffers Meadows or Marshes. Presumably this area was set apart for a section of the community so afflicted. But I can assure you it was nothing of the kind. First of all the word is a county corruption of Duffus, meaning a dovecote and is connected with dows or pigeons. Duffy Dows were young pigeons, not fully fledged; and duffies were pigeons. After all it is so easy to slur a word. So that tract of ground at Middleton, Flemish-like in its willowy beauty, has nothing to do with the mentality of the local inhabitants, but with the craftiest bird that ever flew.

I have just come across a post card of this very area, and to me it appears as old as old can be, certainly no later than the Middle Ages. How it got its name I would not know, because it can have no relationship with dows or pigeons, as they would not have found much to their liking in those meadows. There was an old Suffolk saying about their choice of food:

The dow she dew no sorrow know,
Until she dew a benten go.

Bents, incidentally, is coarse reedy grass that grows along the sandy shore and helps to counteract sea erosion.

But looking back a long way, this tract of land is in a direct line with a rather fine columbarium at Yoxford at Cockfield Hall.

I have always thought it was a bit rough on the poor serf when the Lord of the Manor was allowed to maintain these voracious birds for his table when no meat was available, and let them loose on other peoples' property to obtain their sustenance. Presumably, pigeons were almost sacred, in any case they seem to have a charmed life, always battening on the best crop, particularly peas.

Then when food was scarce they will turn to the succulence of the local gardens. They have been always a menace and the most difficult birds to shoot, possessing almost a second sight. The old country remark is called to mind when out with a gun: 'Lay squat (hidden), hinder come a dow'.

But this picture of a bit of old, old Suffolk holds a good crop of memories. Through the middle of this misty valley runs a small stream that begins as the Yox at Yoxford and changes to the Min at Middleton. It is crossed by a bit of a bridge, all railed in, which shows white against the green. Along its banks, towards evening, groups of boys with long hazel rods could be seen going after eels. It was a rewarding occupation for poor larders, otherwise it would not have been so popular, but after all it was an essentially country pleasure to be classified with birds' nesting and rabbiting. Of course the elders found something a bit more daring, like the old carrier from Blaxhall named Felgate.

He would sidle into a boot-and-shoe shop in Woodbridge and deposit a mysterious sack near the office. And then in nothing of a whisper, audible to all and sundry, announce: 'Nice one in there Mr French — you can have him for five bob!' (Probably a large hare). Or, 'A nice pair of 'em, Mr French. You can have 'em for six shillings.' They were very tasty pheasants or partridges, and awkward questions were not asked, especially as the large estates were so near.

But returning back in time, our little stream must have been a rare venue for smuggling. The crop would be landed at the Sluice, Minsmere or Sizewell, and then ferried along the deserted meadows, with a drop off possibly at the Middleton Rectory and the Westleton Vicarage. In any case the latter has a peculiar little subway leading to the road. After that there was Middleton "Bell", with nothing left behind. One imagines it was a comparatively easy run, provided the moon was right. Middleton Duffers were nearly as artful as the old dows, certainly they knew every twist and turn to achieve their ends.

Duffers Meadows or Marshes announce their age by their fauna. When I knew it there was an abundant crop of wild rhubarb; but it was also noted for king cups or marsh marigolds.

During the last war it was brought under the plough and it has taken all those years since to bring it back again to its own particular growth. Or in the words of an old inhabitant: 'Them thare owd paigles ha' come back again.' So the rhythm of nature asserts itself once more in this wistful portion of an old world.

However, the old lady was a bit wrong in her nomenclature, because paigles are cowslips, not marsh marigolds. They used to provide a delicious glass of duty free aperitif, as all the country side knew, as they did also cowslip balls for the children.

There were also rushes. I wonder how many of those old Suffolk housewives went into those "midders" to get a few to turn them into rushlights? They might burn for an hour if they were long enough.

> Hope, like the gleaming taper's light,
> 　Adorns and cheers our way;
> And still, as darker grows the night,
> 　Emits a brighter ray.

They did not need many, or long, rushlights because when

the sun set they were off to bed as the day started with the dawn, or even earlier.

4

YOXFORD

When gloamin' treads the heels o' day,
And birds sit courin' on the spray,
Alang the flow'ry hedge I stray,
To meet mine ain dear somebody.
                    Robert Tannahill

Although grandfather belonged to his village of Middleton,
grandmother whose maiden name had been Brown, belonged
to Yoxford. Now Middleton church has a little leaded spire
and in the old days a brazen cock on the tidling top, while
Yoxford church has a spire also. When the sun came up out of
the sea the first thing it shone upon was that spire and its bird,
and when it set it seemed to go down behind its brother spire
over yonder.

I have no means of knowing whether grandmother's old
home still stands but one can imagine her playing on its old
brick floor with her kittens before a large open fire. So passed
the few brief days of her childhood. Neither do I know who
taught her to read and write but perchance she knew Jane
Taylor's verse:

O that it were my chief delight
  To do the things I ought!
Then let me try with all my might
  To mind what I am taught.

True, they had an Academy at Yoxford, but I doubt if it was
working in her time, or if it was within the means of the Brown

family. In all probability it was a neighbouring dame, who held her little school in her kitchen, or out in the garden when the weather was kind; because grandmother could write as her old faded letters testify. But I have never seen any of grandfather's writing, although he could sign his name in quite a nice hand.

Perhaps she was helped by a *Play Grammar* by Mrs Corner, or a little visible aid in the shape of a decorated mug just $2\frac{3}{4}$ inches high, with a transfer heading of: 'Adjectives, have three degrees of comparison. Short 1st. Shorter 2nd. Shortest 3rd. Mary is *short*, positive degree 1st. James is *shorter* comparative degree, 2nd. Frank is *shortest* superlative degree 3rd.' Although, I must say, they all look about the same height. In any case this delightful little bit o' larnin' came from Middleton.

I think grandmother was early left an orphan, in any case she had a sister and a brother. How she met grandfather must be left to speculation. I think he was older than her, but in any case it was a love match and the coming together of two opposite temperaments. Grandmother was a brunette amongst a countryside of Saxon complexions, and quietly restrained withal, while grandfather's nature was ebullient. When he went on a frolic it was he who enjoyed the excitement. Perhaps it was that she found a job in Middleton first as a dairymaid, or he a job in Yoxford, a ploughman, turning a furrow and learning his way to the top of his craft. In any case I think his favourite flower must have been honesty, which was also known as "pennyflower" or "money in both pockets"; even "silver pence" when one's purse was always empty. And they settled in Middleton as I have told.

And so my mother came into the world of Suffolk with its abiding memories—their first child.

Not long ago I had a letter from someone who was also born in Middleton and has stayed on satisfied with her lot. This is what she wrote and it might have been my mother's girlhood repeated: 'There were certain things we did each year: March to April we gathered primroses. We went to see the lambs on "Parson's Midder" and looking for robins' nests along the Fen Street banks. Picking cowslips on Theberton Hall Park. Going to look at the Rectory magnolia tree. Visiting Dunwich in the August school holidays. September blackberry picking, and hazel nuts near the Roundhouse. Shuffling through the beech leaves on the road in front of the Rectory and getting old man's beard for the Harvest Festival at the Chapel; and the last fruits—the bullaces.

'The country still has a wintry look—the trees are a network of beech twigs and brambles against a background of grey sky. But the farmers are preparing the land for drilling. Once again there has been a carpet of snowdrops on Taterbilly Eave's marsh, and the primroses are in bloom on the Title Road.'

But to return to grandmother's Yoxford. It was, and is, a village of memories and royal memories at that. It comes last in the Suffolk directories; but in the words of the old Book we are reminded that many that are last shall be first, which in this case would be amongst the first in beauty and peacefulness. Because you do not go to Yoxford to be going anywhere in particular. You sort of meander through and in the old days you could have walked in the middle of the road. If you had been in a reflective mood, not exactly in the elegiac, it might have called to mind that delightful bit of autobiographical description once delivered by a country girl: 'First comes my co-at, then comes my petty co-at, then comes my betty-cum-bob, and then comes Oi!' By which time you would have reached the church.

Clement Scott, who was drama critic for the *Daily Telegraph* and who gave the name "Poppyland" to Cromer and district, called it "Our Village". True, he was given to rather fulsome language and described it as a "garden", but he wrote of it before the famous Three Tuns was burnt down, hence the adulation: "I am inclined to think that the most pleasant feature of our village is the romantic old-world inn, a long, white, low, dormer-windowed, picturesque building, with thick white window frames, and a blue sign swinging over the hospitable door — a real old-fashioned coaching inn, very much in repute fifty years ago, for did not a London coach stop here, was it not watered — and brandy and watered too — on its way to Great Yarmouth. . . . An inn with stables that could accommodate a squadron of cavalry.'

Then his eyes wandered to the other side of the road where: 'I can see a Corisande garden, a garden gay this lovely summer with tall, ivory-white madonna lilies, and branches of magenta phlox, and avenues of roses, and beds of dear old-fashioned sweet william and picotees, and such an undergrowth of mignonette carpeting the old apple and pear trees, that the combined odours perfume this scented village street.' Which brings to a modern mind the question — where has all the mignonette gone to?

Naturally, Yoxford centres about its flint-towered church with its elegant little spire. Within its walls are records of the great families of Brooke and Blois, not omitting a more recent one to Major General S. H. Lomax who led the 1st Division of the B.E.F. into action in the never-to-be forgotten August of 1914. Happily the family of Blois still remain and have amongst their possessions the leather-bound trunk, a pathetic survival of that sad prisoner, Lady Catherine Grey, whose body rested in that church before it was removed to a gorgeous tomb at Salisbury.

I have just come across a delightful picture of a wedding scene at this same church, taken somewhen at the turn of this century. It speaks of serenity with a lovely bride on the arm of her father. I have also discovered that she had been a maid at Middleton rectory and then took up dress-making under a Miss Cotton at Yoxford, hence her simple though beautiful dress. But she would persist in a black hat.

But there is something else in that picture, the memorial on the right to a Wellington Whincop, who was born in June 1815, and so named. The great news must have trickled through in time for the christening, causing so much relief to a countryside that had been all too vulnerable to a fearful threat. Wellington was a whitesmith and grandmother as a little girl must have known him. He was obviously proud of his name. They had cause to be patriotic in those days because undoubtedly some Yoxford lads had been there on that morning.

This charming old photograph shows just one thing more, viz the iron rails that surround the churchyard. There is a note written in the fly-leaf of the registers, a masterpiece of erudition by the Parish Clerk: '200 yards of this iron palacead round the Church yard was begun and finished in the year 1817, and finished the year following 1818, this iron palacead every 3 feet cost 19*s*. 6*d*. it is more than 300 yards in round.' Contradictions notwithstanding. Then comes: 'the last Peal of 700 & 20 rung upon the ground floor in this Tower was for King George the 4th on the 24 of April his birthday being kept on that day 1820. William Barnes, Clerk of the Parish of Yoxford.'

It would appear that when Victoria was Queen an Irishman had his eyes on the living. He wanted to buy the advowson and present himself. He was so sure about things that he came over and had a good look round for somewhere to establish himself. First he picked out The Rookery, rather a nice little estate but which he only viewed from the gateway. He also looked at two other houses in Yoxford, also Kelsale Lodge, which was a nice little canter away.

His mind fastened on The Rookery and negotiations commenced; but he failed to notice that he was expected to buy the furniture as well as the house before he could know that the advowson was fixed. His interview with Lord Stradbroke was badly timed, as his Lordship had just come in from shooting, wet through, and naturally wanted to change his clothes. However, by this time his horses had probably arrived with his men from Ireland. He possessed three carriages, six maids and a well connected wife, together with a family that enjoyed horse riding as much as he did. In fact riding was considered necessary to his health and that was why he looked at Kelsale Lodge.

It must have all fallen through so Yoxford lost this asset to the society of the neighbourhood. He might have left behind so many tales for the locals to tell about the Irish vicar and his horsemanship. Not forgetting that Edgar Wilmot Wright was the veterinary surgeon, held in more respect than the doctor. Besides there was a William Arnold and Edgar Wright, farriers and Edward Dalby, blacksmith.

Yoxford was a much bigger village than Middleton because it had a population of 1,148 at the 1871 census to Middleton's 526. These included a hawker, two farriers as above, two pork butchers, milliner, three tailors, two shoemakers, cattle dealer, carpenter, blacksmith, ironmonger, coal dealer, chemist and dentist, two bakers, two plumbers and glaziers, two butchers (carrying on the tradition set by a forerunner of Cardinal Wolsey there), tea dealer, two builders, saddler and harness maker, stationer and post office, watchmaker and jeweller, colliery agent, coal and salt merchant, who lived at Rose Cottage, and a thatcher. Ephraim Hunt was a cooper, George Nesson a farmer, who was also a brick, tile, drainpipe and pot manufacturer; and an overseer. His home was at Holly Tree Farm. Then there was a wheelwright and blacksmith, a wheelwright and builder, coach builder, two more watchmakers, a boot and shoe manufacturer, a miller and corn merchant, two grocers and drapers, and a furniture broker. Perhaps the most outstanding was William Dennison, confectioner, sodawater, seltzer, potash, lemonade, ginger ale and ginger beer maker. (I have one of his glass marble-stoppered bottles.)

What more could one expect from one so compact and delightfully situated entity, where it was also recorded: 'The peal of bells are new and were hung in September 1879, with new patent clappers called the Redenhall gravitation clapper, the plan causes the clapper to leave the bell directly after impact.'

Of the two doctors it might be said one was an ordinary practitioner who was held in great respect for miles around. He achieved a splendid funeral, his body being taken to the next village of Westleton in a glass-sided hearse and a picture postcard made of the event. I am not sure if it was the same hearse, but a local pedlar of fish managed to buy an old hearse which he used as a travelling shop. He was wont to announce his fish as: "All-alive-O"!

The other doctor was described as surgeon, admiralty surgeon and agent for Misner Haven, with Dunwich detachment. But it was the hoss doctor who had a broadsheet indited in his honour when he died.

A specimen of the work of the carriage builder has survived in a postcard. It is a remarkable testimony of what sort of craftmanship could come out from a village workshop. It speaks for itself of pride in something faithfully done. Its career ended with the coming of the motorcar.

F. J. Punchard, baker and confectioner in the adjoining village of Peasenhall, for whom it was made, could claim descent from the Suffolk branch of an ancient family, who came over with William the Conqueror's armies, from Pontchardon, a village near Neufila in Normandy. Their story has been told in a small book privately printed under the title: *Records of an Unfortunate Family* by E. G. Punchard, D. D. Oxon, Canon of Ely. Their name is on the Battle Abbey Roll.

As an addendum to this chapter I give the Suffolk branch which did not appear in the county until the fifteenth century. The earliest note is of a William Punchard, free tenant of Bedingfield who was an inquisitor at Stonham Court leet in 1464–1492. He died in 1506 and his will is preserved at Ipswich.

John Punchard of Bedingfield married Margaret ffiske of Tyvetshall. She died in 1609 leaving considerable estates to her children. The elder son, Jeremy succeeded in 1621 and had further legacies from his cousin Anne Borret. Jeremy died in 1637, leaving his children in the care of his brother John, who died unmarried in 1659, leaving all his possessions to the family.

The three sons of Jeremy became heads of three separate branches, John, Jeremy and William. John went to Gonville and Caius College, Cambridge and was licensed to the curacy of Aspall, 1674 and Boyton 1674–5. In 1678 he became Rector of Hasketon, where he died in his eighty-fifth year in 1736. He had married Prudence, daughter of the Reverend Robert Camborne, vicar of Campsey Ashe. She died in 1716 leaving seven children. Stephen, the second son, died at Framsden in 1751; he had mortgaged all the Bedingfield lands in 1737, which had come down to him from 1460, and his surviving son, John, was sued by the mortgagee and lost everything.

Of the children of Jeremy, second son of Jeremy, a large family sprang up from Charles the youngest, the most noteworthy being Charles of Pakenham (1804–1864), a famous breeder of fowls.

A John Punchard, eldest son of John Punchard and Rachael Carter was born at Easton in 1686 and died at Hacheston in his seventieth year. He married Mary, daughter of Francis and Mary Folkhard of Parham, who received under her father's will various lands at Peasenhall. John their only son was born at Saxtead in 1728. He hired several farms, including Parham Hall and did much to improve the breed of horses and cattle, including the Suffolk horses known as "Punches", a corruption according to the record of "Punchard". But the fact remains that in the story of the Suffolk horse there is no reference to the Punchard family. He died in 1787.

John Baldry Punchard, born at Saxtead in 1766, succeeded to the Peasenhall estates. He married Rose Elgood of Cransford in 1792. Within six years the Peasenhall estates had to be sold. Rose died at Framlingham in her ninety-eighth year in 1872.

Survivors of this prolific family, who spread all over the county, with connections at Witnesham, Dennington, Eye, Easton, Burgate, Ipswich, Framsden, Coddenham, Bramford,

Stonham, Henly, Hemingstone, Chelmondiston, are still to be found. But why the doctor should describe his record as that of 'an unfortunate family' is hard to explain.

In Loving Memory of
EDGAR WILLMOTT WRIGHT, M.R.C.V.S.
For many years Veterinary Surgeon at Yoxford
Died Friday, 26th July 1912
Interred at Yoxford Cemetery, Monday, 29th July

We have lost our old Veterinary Doctor,
He has passed o'er the boundary of life,
Free from his pain and his suffering,
Gone from all sorrow and strife.
His form and his voice we'll remember,
For he spoke with no uncertain sound,
And many there'll be who will miss him,
All over the countryside round.

Many years he has practised amongst us,
Not a cleverer veterinary here,
So prompt to attend to each summons,
Let the call come from far or from near.
And for miles around they'd send for our Doctor,
No matter whatever the cost,
For his skill was well known with the horses,
He so seldom an animal lost.

Dr Wright was a little bit blustering,
If you riled him, Oh! how he would swear!
But still for all that he was generous,
He'd a heart that could feel and would care,
And should a poor man need assistance,
Not a more willing helper than he,
And many an action of kindness,
For ever remembered will be.

For months Dr Wright was a sufferer,
Though bravely he tried to defy,
A cruel complaint that attacked him,
But at last was compelled to lay by.
And now he has passed o'er the river,
To the great Master's will we must bend,
Yet we'll join with his sorrowing loved ones,
And mourn for a comrade and friend.

In the grave dark and cold, they have laid him,
And mourners from far and from near,
To the cemetery followed his coffin,
By his grave-side to drop a last tear.
Beneath the green turf we have left him,
Amid scenes of respect all around,
There he'll sleep on in peace till the morning,
Until the last trump shall sound.

By W. S. Montgomery,
Blind Organ Grinder, WESTLETON.

5

A YOXFORD EXERCISE BOOK

> Multiplication is vexation
> Division is as bad
> The Rule of three perplexes me
> And Practice drives me mad

I have just come across a nicely bound little book of Arithmetrical Exercises which belonged to a Master C. Rayner of Middleton, who attended C. P. Jonas's Academy at Yoxford, 30th September 1869. He could not have been very old; evidently his father was dead because his mother ran the farm at Fordley Hall and his brother another farm at Falkenham.

The exercises are written in the prescribed copper plate, and were evidently designed for the education of a farmer-to-be. They start with Practice, 'so called from the general use thereof by all persons concerned in trade and business . . . .'.

All questions in this rule are performed by taking aliquot or even parts, by which means many tedious reductions are avoided, the Table of which is as follows . . .

Rule 1. When the price is less than a penny divide by the aliquot parts that are in a penny then by 12 and 20, which will give the answer.

Rule 2. When the price is less than a Shilling take the aliquot part or parts that are in a shilling, add them together and divide by 20 as before.

Rule 3. When the price is more than one shilling and less than two. ˙

Rule 4. If the price be an even number of shillings under 20 — multiply the quantity by half the number, doubling the first figure of the product for shillings, and the rest will be pounds.

Rule 5. When the price consists of odd Shillings. . . .

Rule 6. When the price is Shillings and pence. . . .

Rule 7. When the price is Pounds and Shillings. . . .

Rule 8. When the price and quantity given are of several denominations, multiply the price by the integers, and take parts of the price for the lower denominations.

So follows exercises in the price of cheese, molasses, pearl ashes (what could they have been?), butter, madder, hops, Malaga raisins, Zante currants, sugar, Dutch madder and soap.

Next comes Tare and Tret:

Tare is an allowance made to the Buyer for the weight of the box, barrell, bag etc. At so much per cwt or per 100 lb. At so much the gross weight.

Tret is an allowance of 4 lb in every 104 lb or 1/26th for waste, dust etc made by the merchant to the buyer.

Cloff is an allowance of 2 lb for every 3 cwt or 1/60th part for waste on a few articles, but is now very seldom made.

Commission follows next, with Brokerage, Insurance, Stocks (public funds) and Interest; leading to Proportion. . . .

If 236 men eat 160 qr of Wheat in 102 days, how much will 76 men eat in 1 year 67 days?

Simple Interest and Fractions need no comment. But I must say that Master Rayner kept his book remarkably neat and tidy. It ends in a few blank pages which he puts to good use for making farming notes, such as:

'Stack Measuring for Long Stacks, Length multiplied by Over equals Feet. Round Stacks. Multiply half the distance round the Eaves by the Over, gives the answer. Charles Rayner signs this October 9th, 1873.'

Now follows a personal note: 'In the year 1880 our Haysell weather was very wet. In the above named year my Friend William Catton died. I went to Church on the Sunday morning to hear his Funeral Sermon preached, was by the Revnd George Hamilton. The day was by no means fine, very heavy storms passed over in the afternoon; my Sister Jane went to

(above) Duffers Meadows, Middleton, and *(below)* a Suffolk
yeoman's home at Capel, now demolished

E.B. Fisher's shop, Yoxford

A Yoxford bride

(above) the Prim Methodist chapel, Yoxford, and *(below)*
a carriage built at Yoxford

Joseph Broom who began as a hawker (*see opposite*), was first postmaster of Middleton-cum-Fordley. The office remained in his family for nearly a century

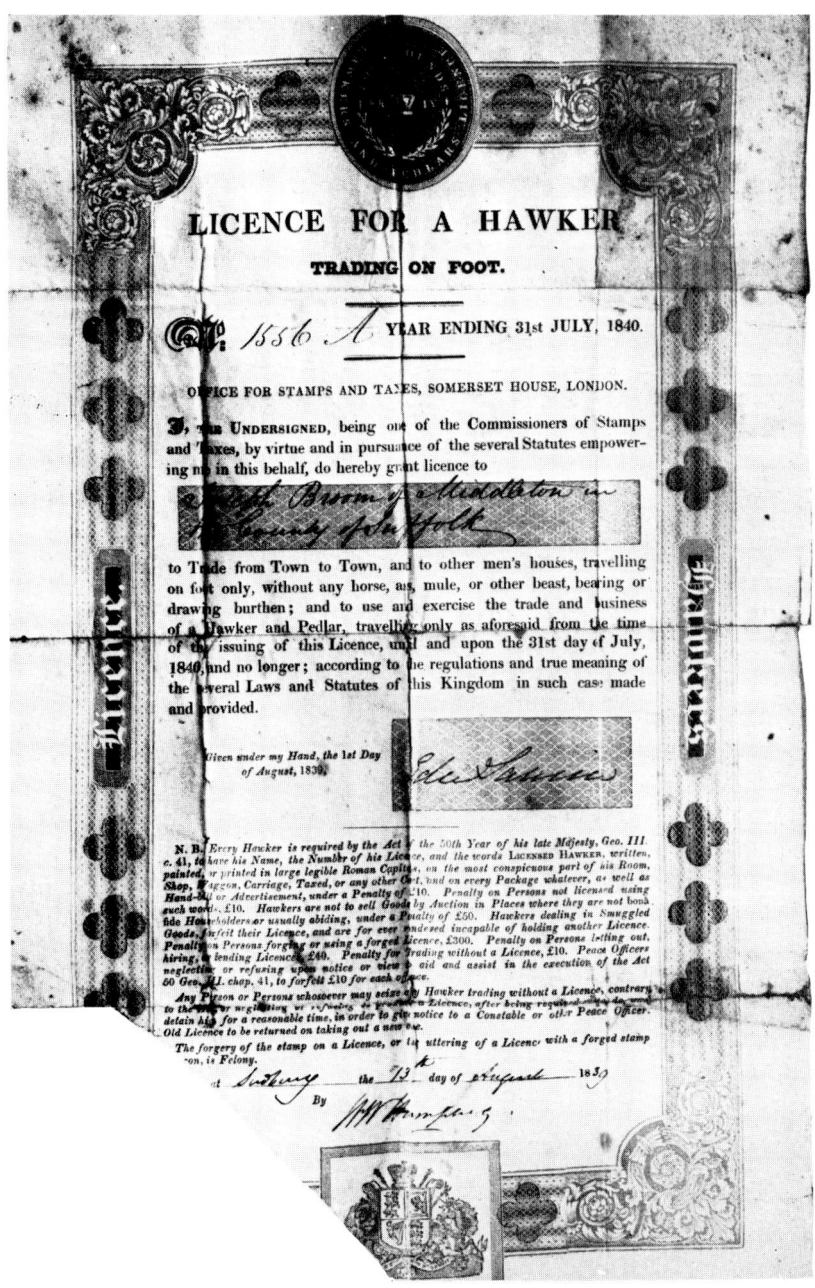

LICENCE FOR A HAWKER
TRADING ON FOOT.

№ *1556* A YEAR ENDING 31st JULY, 1840.

OFFICE FOR STAMPS AND TAXES, SOMERSET HOUSE, LONDON.

I, THE UNDERSIGNED, being one of the Commissioners of Stamps and Taxes, by virtue and in pursuance of the several Statutes empowering me in this behalf, do hereby grant licence to *Joseph Broom of Middleton in the County of Suffolk*

to Trade from Town to Town, and to other men's houses, travelling on foot only, without any horse, ass, mule, or other beast, bearing or drawing burthen; and to use and exercise the trade and business of a Hawker and Pedlar, travelling only as aforesaid from the time of the issuing of this Licence, until and upon the 31st day of July, 1840, and no longer; according to the regulations and true meaning of the several Laws and Statutes of this Kingdom in such case made and provided.

Given under my Hand, the 1st Day of August, 1839,

N. B. *Every Hawker is required by the Act of the 50th Year of his late Majesty, Geo. III. c. 41, to have his Name, the Number of his Licence, and the words* LICENSED HAWKER, *written, painted, or printed in large legible Roman Capitals, on the most conspicuous part of his Room, Shop, Waggon, Carriage, Tazed, or any other Cart, and on every Package whatever, as well as Hand-Bill or Advertisement, under a Penalty of £10. Penalty on Persons not licensed using such words, £10. Hawkers are not to sell Goods by Auction in Places where they are not bonâ fide Householders or usually abiding, under a Penalty of £50. Hawkers dealing in Smuggled Goods, forfeit their Licence, and are for ever rendered incapable of holding another Licence. Penalty on Persons forging or using a forged Licence, £200. Penalty on Persons letting out, hiring, or lending Licences, £40. Penalty for Trading without a Licence, £10. Peace Officers neglecting or refusing upon notice or view to aid and assist in the execution of the Act 50 Geo. III. chap. 41, to forfeit £10 for each offence.*

Any Person or Persons whatsoever may seize any Hawker trading without a Licence, contrary to the said Act, or neglecting or refusing to produce a Licence, after being required so to do, and detain him for a reasonable time, in order to give notice to a Constable or other Peace Officer. Old Licence to be returned on taking out a new one.

The forgery of the stamp on a Licence, or the uttering of a Licence with a forged stamp thereon, is Felony.

at *Sudbury* the 13th day of *August* 1839

By

Leiston school in the eighteen-eighties

Providence House,
Peasenhall

Euston Hall, the
seat of the Duke of
Grafton

His Highness the Maharajah Duleep Singh

Captain Pretyman's reception in Orwell Park, 1894

Church leaving me house keeper, Mother staying at my Brother Jonathans at Faulkenham the same time! Charles Robert Rayner Dated this 4 day of July 1880 Sunday afternoon.' I am afraid that Charles was not much of a scholar, so I have added a little punctuation to make the essay a little clearer.

The copy of a lease is made by another hand and is not without interest considering the times in which it was drawn up;

The lessors agree to let the lessees who agree to hire of the lessors the Farm lands and premises at Middleton & Yoxford comprised in an indenture of Lease dated the first day of June 1878 and made between Hooper John Wilkinson Esq and Anne his wife both since deceased of the one part and the Lessees of the other part from the eleventh day of Oct. next for the term of four years, determined in the event hereinafter mentioned at the yearly rent of £156.16s.0d. and in all other respect upon the same terms as the said farm and lands are now held by the Lessees under the said lease except as herinafter mentioned. And it is agreed that a lease shall be forthwith executed Lessors and Lessees in pursuance of this agreement upon the request of either party and at their joint expense, and it is further agreed that the yearly rent of £156.16s.0d. shall date back to Michaelmas last and be paid as the rent for the said premises for the current year instead of the rent of £275 reserved by the said existing lease the reservation of game in the existing lease shall except hereinafter mentioned be considered as struck out and Lessees shall have the exclusive right to Game and Rabbits in plantations adjoining the said farms and not adjoining Mr Reads Farm. If during the lease the Rookery Mansion shall be let to a resident occupier desiring to have the game on the estate shall be sold then such reservation as aforesaid shall from the commencement of such letting or from the completion of such sale as the case may be come into force and the Lessees shall be entitled to a reduction of the said rent to the extent of £7.0s.0d. or a proportionate part thereof for a part of the year. That if Louisa Rayner shall die before the eleventh day of October 1888 then the lease hereby agreed upon shall expire on the eleventh day of October next but one after her death. Witness the hands of the said parties.

The following is of interest of work done with terms used that went out with the use of the horse:

Long Meadow 8½ acres for beet. Wheat Stubble ploughed in five bouts. Harrowed twice in a place with heavy harrows two horses and a man. Muck 130 loads. Spreading 5s. an acre. Rolling twice, one horse roll before and after drill. Harrowing three times. Drilling 34 lb of beet seed, fifteen bags beet manure sown, but crop failed. Ploughed in five bouts, drilled 5 acres, swedes. Harrowed twice. Rolled twice. Horse hoed twice. Furrows cut out with furrow hoe. Swedes chopped out and singled. 15 acres work one man.

To Messrs Flick & Son. Grassy Field 4¾ acres. Ploughed in four bouts. Close warded, warded back & drawn out and stacked.

Stackyard field 6 acres. 3½ acres turnips.

4-acre part Wheat stubble ploughed on steach [*sic*]. Warded up close and well, harrowed up and down and acrost [*sic*]. Warded back. Scarified twice. Cultivated once. Harrowed once, drawed out, mucked thirty-six carts, part. Ploughed up for turnips, rolled, harrowed once, drilled turnips, Rolled once one acre quarter more turnips drilled, twenty carts muck, Horse hoed twice. Turnips set out and singled.

2-acre part. Ploughed up in five bouts.

2-acre part. Ploughed back in five bouts.

2-acre part. Ploughed back in five bouts.

Scarified once, harrowed once. Ploughed in five bouts. Ploughed in five bouts, Oct.

This farming record calls to mind tales about some of the old hands, and their love of the work. There was a man named Chaston who lived at Middleton about the time of this record. The farmer he worked for gave him a day's holiday. His immediate reaction was: 'Thank ee master, I'll drive them ship ta market for ya!' That was his idea of a day off.

Then there was old Will Wasp, pronounced Warsp, who used to walk four or five miles to work. He would walk into the farm kitchen with his hat on, sit down at the table and remark: 'I'm riddy fur me breakfast, Ma'am.' And she, good woman that she was, saw that he had one.

Again there were two old farmers named Button and Clutton, who were rare pals. They used to greet one another: 'Mornin Mr Button!' 'Mornin Mr Clutton!'

One of them was thrashing peas so the other enquired as to how they were coming out?

'Rare quietly', was the reply. 'I put nine coomb in an' I ha only gort eight coomb out! I wonder where that dratted owd coomb gort to?' (It should have been a coomb an acre,)

6

UNWILLINGLY TO SCHOOL

And then the whining schoolboy, with his satchel,
And shining morning face, creeping like snail
Unwillingly to school.

I started my scholastic career at a dame school, but it was
never so crowded as the subject of my picture, although it was
held in a private house as in this case. When you come to look
closely into the photograph it seems extraordinary that so
many tots could be gathered into so small a space and remain
still until the man under the black cloth replaced the cap.

There they sit, arms folded, as by ancient custom to bring
order and discipline to the rather large class. When they grew
older they probably had to fold their arms behind them. And
to those who were young a generation or two afterwards; do
you remember the order — 'arms folded and heads on desks'? I
wonder if the house still stands or like Cowper's school — ''tis
now become a history little known'.

Somewhere about the fifties of last century one of Lady
Bunbury's duties at Mildenhall was to visit the school, hear the
children recite their lessons and answer her questions in order
that the headmaster should receive his efficiency pay. It is said
that one year the unfortunate man did not pass the test.

It is a long time now since children learned their tables and
to recite, but the latter often left a memory of splendid English
that lasted a lifetime. I was asked sometime ago if I could give
the origin of a delightful little poem on trees. I asked a local
headmistress, who looked up and replied — 'Oh, I learned that
by heart when I was at school'. She then went on to say that

children are not taught that way now.

Suffolk women were in the van for juvenile learning. Anne Laetitia Barbould, Mrs Trimmer, and Elizabeth Bonhote, who was the daughter of James Mapes, baker of Earsham Street, Bungay. She married Daniel Bonhote, a solicitor, and about 1787, while in bad health she wrote for her children's guidance, a series of moral essays called *The Parental Monitor*.

Discipline was heavy in those old days, with the birch and the cane always in attendance. One boy at the famous Edward VI Bury School was punished with 2,000 lines in a week, while the forms allowance that week was 23,450. This was partly solved by the ingenious device of tying one pen above another. They had a master named Carpenter and when at a loose end the boy in question would draw pictures of the Walrus and the Carpenter. He was caught at this pastime on one occasion and made to stay in and draw twenty copies of the offending picture. Fortunately for him a friend came to his assistance.

One of the amusements in the classroom was the making of inkqueducts, by cutting a channel on the desks and upsetting the ink down this. The fluid was then directed to the edge of the desk and cascaded to the floor where it made a most satisfactory mess.

But this was a famous school producing famous men of whom Edward Fitz-Gerald was one. It is said that in the early days the masters had to appoint two boys as censors to note offenders, but then secretly they had to detail another boy to watch the behaviour of the censors.

Returning to the children in the picture, all of whom are respectably dressed, they are of the new generation of compulsory education. They were infinitely better off than their fathers and mothers. The church schools had done much and the chapels also, the latter teaching reading and writing in their Sunday Schools.

When Queen Victoria came to the throne it was said that less than half the population of Suffolk could read. But organizations such as the National Society for the Education of the Poor in the Principles of the Established Church and the British and Foreign School Society, which was largely supported by the Nonconformists, were at work. Then came the Forster Act which led on to the Board Schools, School Attendance Committees and the School Inspectors, known as H.M.I.s. In 1880 school attendance became compulsory up to the age of thirteen, but exemptions were possible at ten, raised to eleven in 1893 and twelve in 1889. The inspectors of the time stated that the opponents of public elementary education were the farmers. Another factor was the employment of children to earn a little money for the upkeep of the family.

The 1870 Act was passed during the payment-by-results system, which was instituted in 1862. This was a hard test for the children and teachers, and turned the H.M.I. into a bogey. The inspector would appoint a day and examine the children. They had to do three or four sums, read a passage from one or two set books for reading and do a short spelling test, and a piece of dictation for writing.

A. J. Swinburne, one of the Suffolk Inspectors said: 'For weeks beforehand the children were stuffed and almost roasted, the mistresses had sleepless nights, the parson and the squire of the village were in a flutter of anxiety, for so much depended at that time on the verdict of Her Majesty's Inspector.' He also told of the Blundeston mistress who collapsed in a dead faint, because she thought the H.M.I. was failing her small charges.

Payments by results disappeared after 1895, but it had its good influences as well as its bad. For one thing it improved reading, although the H.M.I. for the Ipswich area said in 1881: 'I am almost prepared to admit that a boy may read perfectly well, though I may not be able to understand a single word.' So the old Suffolk dialect was not affected. But the strain on the children was exemplified by a little girl in Bungay, named Florence Porter who would get up in her sleep and work out sums on the wall and cry out.

Then came the Passive Resisters of 1903, when prominent Nonconformists refused to pay their rates, caused by the passing of the Education Act of 1902. And this is what a Christian minister in Bury St Edmunds could exclaim: 'If any priests, Anglican or Romish, wish to teach their particular dogmas to anybody's children, let them do so, if they like to pay for it, but to compel a Protestant to help pay for the teaching is unmitigated impudence. Let them have teachers of their errors if they wish, but not at my expense.'

Bury St Edmunds was the first town in East Anglia where resisters were brought before the Bench, and also the first place where their goods were put up for auction. The first sale, held in the Constitutional Club in July 1903 almost caused a riot. Crowds thronged into the hall and outside in Guildhall Street. When the goods were sold most of them were bought by other passive resisters and returned to their owners. So all in all it was a stupid business.

At Sudbury, out of ten resisters summoned in one day, six were women and two of the four were J.P.'s. Orders for payments were made, with distraint in default. At a demonstration held afterwards in the Market Hall, one minister said they were prepared to rot in gaol rather than submit to the Act. This sectarian war lasted some years and then died a well merited natural death.

Turning to a cognate subject which has an amusing side, when the Welfare State was born and the National Insurance Act was passed, the first Insurance baby that attracted most attention in Ipswich, was the son of an employee of Ransomes, Sims and Jefferies, St Peter's Works. The father's shopmates presented Dad with a cradle.

Another early arrival, somewhere between midnight and 1 a.m. on 14th January 1913, was a son of a member of the Ancient Order of Foresters. Without waiting for daylight, the excited father rushed off to the local secretary, roused him out of bed, in order to learn how he could obtain the thirty-shillings he had become entitled to.

7

GARRETT'S IRON WORKS, LEISTON

The machines that are first invented to perform any particular movement are always the most complex, and succeeding artists generally discover that with fewer wheels, with fewer principles of motion than had originally been employed, the same effects may be more easily produced. The first philosophical systems, in the same manner, are always the most complex.   Adam Smith.

A near neighbour of grandfather's Middleton, was the Leiston Works. And this is an extract from the *Suffolk Garland* of 1866.

THIS IS TO INFORM THE PUBLIC

That whereas I, Richard Garret, of Woodbridge (Late of Ufford), in the county of Suffolk, Blade-smith, have always stamped my Sickles and other Edge-tools with my name, R. Garret, and have acquired, by using the best steel and great care in workmanship, a large demand for my wares (especially Sickles and Hoes); but my name, R. Garret, has of late been counterfeited, and stamped on sale Sickles and Hoes by some bad person or persons in or near Sheffield, in Yorkshire, and been sold wholesale to several shops in Norwich, Yarmouth, Harleston, Diss, Beccles, Bungay, Halesworth, Lowestoft, and many other towns and country shops, which Sickles and Hoes have been retailed for my make at Eighteen-pence each (the price of mine are sold at) to Farmers and poor Labourers, when such Sickles and Hoes ought not to be sold for more than Fourteen-pence each, and profit sufficient for an honest man.

Now for preventing such an imposition on the Public and prejudice to myself I have added a star to my former Mark on my Sickles and Hoes &c and am resolved the law shall determine

whether such Makers and Sellers have a right to act as above
without being punished as cheats and counterfeits.   R. Garret

From *Ipswich Journal* of 1765:

The origin of Leiston Works is dated from 1778, in which year
the son of the above-named Richard Garrett [*sic*] went from
Woodbridge and commenced business at Leiston in the trade
followed by his father, *viz*. Sickle and Edge-tool Maker and Blade
Smith. He employed a wheel worked by a single horse, to draw a
grindstone, and had at most from eight to ten men. The business
did not increase beyond this in his time.

He was succeeded by his son in 1805, who in his turn
relinquished the works in favour of the present head of the firm in
1836, and died the year after. He, as well as his father and grandfather, excelled in the production of tools used in husbandry,
though till the year 1806 the sickle was the chief instrument of
their manufacture. At this period Mr Garrett engaged in making
a threshing machine, patented by Mr John Ball of Hetheringsett,
near Norwich, the first of its kind that was fully applied to
threshing purposes in this country. This was considered a serious
undertaking for one in Mr Garrett's humble position, but as the
speculation succeeded beyond the most sanguine expectations of
the patentee, it brought both him and the manufacturer into
great repute amongst the agriculturalists of the Eastern counties
of England.

By which time my grandfather was a little boy and was
brought up to use the flail.

As all the world knows, Garretts (as the name was later
spelt) grew and grew, so that everything made of iron seemed
to come out of their yards. The first traction engines were
superb little bits, puffing away along our quiet roads, and it is
hardly surprising that when their day was done, they became
collectors' pieces. Only as recently as September 1976 came
this bit of news in the *Daily Telegraph*.

Sir Peter Allen, a former chairman of I.C.I., now President
of the Transport Trust, discovered a rare Garrett steamroller
"retired" as far away as Ibiza, and arranged for its transport

back to Britain.

The roller, which burns either wood or coal, is thought to be the only survivor which has "cotton reel" steering — a remarkable system of chains and pulleys that provide its drive. It was one of three sold to Spanish companies in 1923 by the Richard Garrett company of Leiston, Suffolk.

Its recovery has been a model of cooperation. The Spanish Ambassador here persuaded his Ministry of Works to donate the roller to the Trust, I.C.I. helped transport it across Spain and a Spanish company, Aznar Lines ferried it to Southampton without charge. It is now in Peterborough being restored.

8

TWELVE MILES FROM IPSWICH

Dear bells! how sweet the sound of village bells
When on the undulating air they swim!
Now loud as welcomes! faint, now, as farewells.

Hood

I wonder who was the young lady who drew this charming vignette of Wickham Market, for a lady it must have been, since no man could have achieved such taste. And it must have been in a drawing-room as an elegant occupation. Was she pleased when she saw it in print and did it come from Mr Pawsey's shop in Ipswich? But there is more to it than the actual delineation, because she has captured the atmosphere of the times.

Wickham Market is described as being on the old Yarmouth Road, and as a neat and pleasant village. Further, 'the church which stands on high ground affords the most extensive prospect in the county, for fifty churches may be counted from it.' Moreover, it was a sea-mark telling the old mariners they were nearer Slaughden Quay than Dunwich.

But it is the scene itself that is so fascinating. The women with their poke bonnets that seemed to make even a plain face comely and coy. The wide and dusty road along which the *Shannon* might pass at any minute, sounding its horn if approaching, but silent if departing. The little "owd dawg", sweet Carlo, or some unattached mongrel; and the traveller in the middle of the road, since there were no paths and no danger from passing traffic. It may have been the squire or vicar on horseback, or possibly the doctor saying: 'Put out yare tongue, Bor'!

It must be summer in spite of the smoke from the chimneys, because there was always a fire burning on those old Suffolk hearths. The houses nestle so quietly under their rose red roofs, while the trees add their shade to that noble spire. I do not know whether to suggest it is a Mary Mitford village or a Cranford; perhaps it is an amalgam of the two. It is quite evident that somewhere in those quiet homes lived little old ladies, retired captains, a doctor and one or two bachelors who would have made a hand at loo or cribbage, denoting 'a clear fire, a clean hearth, and the rigour of the game'.

What did they talk about? Could it have been scandal? After all, Lord Nelson had said himself that Boney might have a go at Hollesley Bay, which was rather near. However, if he did the old ladies were sure that His Grace the Duke of Hamilton and Brandon, K.T. would put him to rights. Miss Matty was quite sure of that and refused to be disturbed by any alarmist rumours. So she went peacefully to bed after saying her prayers, blew out her candle; because she needed no 'drowsy syrops of the world' to woo her to 'that sweet sleep'.

The old church with its extremely beautiful octagon tower and its slender spire has a ring of six bells, the tenor of which caused some disturbance, as the inscription records. 'The monument of Grey is past awaie, In place of it doth stand, The name of John Brend, 1657.' Indeed, that beautiful old shrine has stood for so much of peace and war, because in the registers this bit of joy can be found: 'John the Sonne of John Bachen gent, & Alice his wife was born the 22 April being Easter Day and was baptised the 8th day of May, being the same day whereon our Soveraigne Lord Charles the 2nd was solemnly proclaimed of England, Scotland, ffrance and Ireland, King, Defender of the fayth.' And just as that sanctus bell was removed to the spire for all to see, so it is there today, a wonderful reminder of times lost. True that octagon tower looms out from yesterday, clear and defined, a little out of proportion perhaps in the sketch, but certainly lost as one approaches the old landmark, tucked away as it is in a Suffolk loke (lane). Now it is bypassed and the old narrow street with its houses is saved from being shaken to pieces by heavy traffic.

We must not forget that here was a market as its name implied and that once a week at least it was a babel of tongues, the lowing of cattle, bleating of sheep and the suspicious grunting of pigs. Then, after harvest would come those old Suffolk wagons of blue and red, and occasionally a morphadite. The horses with their ring of bells, martingales and millinery, bearing loads of barley for the maltings, or corn for the miller. For it was and is in the midst of fine farming country and a once poppy-laden air.

The principal hostlery is the "White Hart", which in 1855 was kept by a Susan Chase. But in those now far away times there were other inns and taverns such as "Chaise and Pair", kept by Mary Foreman, "Chequers" by Elizabeth Nichols, "Crown" by Jeremiah Woods, "George" by George Turtel, "Vine" by William Jackson. Mail carts ran daily to Woodbridge, Yarmouth, Stradbroke, Orford etc; and Daniel Mayhew was the carrier to Woodbridge daily; presumably in one of those old covered wagons with dished wheels, laden with people and parcels.

Coming down the years, in 1879 Mr James White of this town had in operation a self-winding clock 'which determined the time with great accuracy, maintaining a consistent motion by itself, never requiring to be wound up and which will continue its movements so long as the component parts exist'.

In those days Messrs Whitmore and Binyon has 'a great reputation for the production of steam engines, water wheels, windmills and machinery, and more especially such as are adapted for corn and flour mills. . . . The several branches of millwrighting, engine fitting, boiler making, iron and brass foundry, mill stones, building (including also the manufacture of improved machines for dressing flour through silk) are all carried on in their several departments . . . the works being supplied with gas manufactured on the premises, and giving employment to a large number of hands.'

Wickham Market was the home of John Kirby from 1732 until his death in 1753. He was the author of *The Travellers Guide and Topographical Description of The County of Suffolk* from actual survey. As a companion piece on the title page is a delightful little vignette, showing what I take to be a tollgate, with a man on a white horse and another on foot; and a leaning signpost that points to Wickham Market. Set in scenery more like Cumberland than Suffolk 'Woodbridge. Printed and sold by Smith and Jarrold.'

What has come to be termed the last gipsy family—the Barhams—lived at Wickham Market. He could neither read nor write, but could count. They were held in sufficient esteem to have a Barham Way on a new estate named after them—on the spot where their caravan rested.

A local inhabitant told me (in 1976): 'When I married forty years ago I bought a couple of dozen pegs off them, and they are still in use.'

I have often thought that the little township would make such a fine setting for a modern picture of the Angelus, so vibrant is the air.

9

THE PEASENHALL MURDER

I don't want anybody to come and tell me as there's been more
going on nor the Prayer-book's got a service for.

Mrs Dollop in *Middlemarch*

The Peasenhall Murder, committed one stormy night of 31st
May and 1st June 1902, has become for all time the Peasenhall
Mystery. That it was murder of a most dastardly kind, that it
was perpetrated by a Peasenhall man, are incontrovertible
facts. It is equally certain that it will never be solved. Time has
sealed it within the passing years.

The victim was a Rose Harsent, a young woman of twenty-
two, a servant in one of the larger houses in Peasenhall, known
as Providence House. She was also a member and constant
worshipper at Sibton Primitive Methodist Chapel and a
member of the choir.

The accused was a William Gardiner, a local man, foreman
carpenter at Smyth's agricultural engineering works at Peasenhall. He was also a member at Sibton Chapel, an office bearer,
Sunday School superintendent, choir master and a man held
in much respect. Sibton, it should be mentioned, is the next
village on the Yoxford side.

The unfortunate Rose was an attractive country girl and
acted as general maid to two elderly people, a Mr and Mrs
Crisp. Mr Crisp was deaf, and they were a quiet retiring
couple who kept themselves to themselves. Rose occupied a
room at the top of the house, which had a separate staircase
running up to it from the kitchen. She was therefore more or

less isolated from the Crisps. Her bedroom had one small window that looked down on the village street. This then was the *mise en scène*.

William Gardiner was a married man with six children. He was described as 'A man of middle stature, with a black beard and whiskers, closely cropped and black hair waved back upon a high forehead'. He was forty-odd years of age. Rose Harsent and the Gardiners were on quite friendly terms.

About a year before the murder, two youths noticed Ruth go into the little chapel, and soon after Gardiner followed. The two young men, George Wright and Alphonso Skinner, became suspicious and silently drew near the door for the purpose of eavesdropping. It should be mentioned that this foxing business was no uncommon pastime in the village life of those days, when there was so little to direct their minds into better channels.

These two youths, no worse than others in those times, alleged they heard Rose cry out, 'Oh, oh!' and later, 'I must be going', or 'You must let me go'. There is supposed to have been more to it than that. It was not long before this bit of scandal was broadcast around the village. Naturally enough, Gardiner had to do something about it.

About a week later he sent for Skinner, who also worked at Smyth's, asking him to come to the foreman's office. He then confronted Skinner as to what it was all about, and why he had set about such a false tale in motion. When Skinner told him what he had heard, Gardiner denied it all, and accused him of telling a pack of lies. 'I know what I saw, Mr Gardiner,' replied Skinner, 'and I know what I heard'.

Gardiner then asked for an apology, otherwise he would put the matter in the hands of a solicitor. He did not get an apology.

This matter naturally got to the ears of the chapel authorities and a meeting was called for 11th May at Sibton Chapel, when Wright and Skinner both attended. Mr John Guy, the superintendent minister from Halesworth, was also in attendance. He had always held a high opinion of Gardiner, but was naturally alarmed when he received a letter from a Mr Rouse, an elderly member of the congregation, telling him of the rumours that were going about. Rose Harsent was not asked to attend, but many of the older members of the congregation were present, as this scandal had reflected badly on the chapel. The two youths were asked to give their version of the story, which they did. Questions were asked but they did not in any way deviate from the original tale.

Gardiner was then called. He declared the tale was a complete fabrication. He was, he said, living happily with his wife and family. He had never taken part in any love affair with Rose Harsent. Although Rose did not attend, as one would have thought she should have done, it appears that Mr Guy had seen her out walking with her mother. He tackled her about the matter, but she denied that anything had taken place between them.

At the conclusion of the meeting, Mr Guy advised Gardiner to go to a solicitor and have a letter sent to the youths, which Gardiner agreed to do. But the minister added, 'I would say that you had better be very careful in future. I hope this will be a lesson to you all your life. I am not saying you have done anything wrong, but you have been indiscreet.'

Gardiner acted on the minister's advice and a letter was sent to each of them as follows:

Halesworth, Suffolk,
15th May 1901.

'Sir,
    Mr William George Gardiner of Peasenhall has consulted me in reference to certain slanderous statements which he alleges you have uttered and circulated concerning him and a young woman. I have to inform you that unless you tender my Client an ample written apology within seven days from this

date legal proceedings will be forthwith commenced against you without further notice to yourself.

Yours faithfully,

Harold A. Mullins'

Neither Wright nor Skinner was intimidated by this. They had told the truth and would stand by it. They did not apologize, neither was any further action taken by Gardiner.

At the time of the enquiry at Sibton Chapel, Gardiner sent Rose two letters:

'Dear Rose,

I was much surprised this morning to hear that there's some scandal going around about you and me going into Doctor's Chapel for immoral purposes so that I shall put it into other hands at once as I have found out who started it. Bill Wright and Skinner say they saw us there but I shall summons them for deformation [*sic*] of character unless they withdraw what they have said and give me a written apology. I shall see Bob tonight and we will come and see you together if possible. I shall at the same time see your father and tell him. Yours etc.

William Gardiner.'

The other letter read:

'Dear Rose,

I have broken the news to Mrs Gardiner this morning, she is awfully upset but she say she know it is wrong, for I was at home from ½ past nine o'clock, so I could not possibly be with you an hour so she won't believe anything about it. I have asked Mr Burgess to ask those two chaps to come to chapel tonight and have it out there however they stand by such a tale I don't know but I don't think God will forsake me now and if we put our trust in Him it will end all right, but its awfully hard work to have to face people when they are all suspicious of you but by Gods help whether they believe me or not I shall try and live it down and prove by my future conduct that it's all false. I only wish I could take it to court but I don't see a shadow of a chance to get the case as I don't think you would be strong enough to face a trial. Trusting that God will direct us and make the way clear — I remain, yours in trouble.

W. Gardiner.'

Both of these letters were in Rose's possession at the time of her death a year later. This seems to suggest the letters were of value and importance to her.

A member of the chapel, Henry Rouse, a labourer, working at Sibton, was suspicious of both Gardiner and Rose. He spoke of seeing them walking out together in the dusk on several occasions. He said he bade them 'Good night' on one such occasion, but they did not reply. This was sometime after the chapel meeting. He also alleged that he saw Gardiner with his feet in Rose's lap when he was preaching on one occasion at Sibton chapel. He sent a letter to Gardiner as a result:

'Mr Gardiner,
    I write to warn you of your conduct with that girl Rose, as I find when she come to chapel she must place herself next to you, which keeps the people's minds still in the belief that you are a guilty man, and in that case you will drive many from the chapel, and those who would join the cause are kept away through it. We are told to shun the least appearance of evil. I do not wish you to leave God's house, but there must be a difference before God's cause can prosper, which I hope you will see to be right as people cannot hear when the enemy of souls bring this before them. I write as one that loves your soul, and I hope you will have her sit in some off place, and remove such feeling which for your sake she will do.'

There was therefore something between Rose and Gardiner,

because when the murder was discovered suspicion immediately rested on him. It was also proved that Rose's younger brother, Henry Harsent, fourteen years of age, had acted as an intermediary between them. He was also employed at the drill works and sometimes Gardiner would ask him to take a letter to his sister. Rose on occasions, gave him replies to take back.

Rose's father, William Harsent, was also employed at the drill works. He was a carter. At the trials he was not asked to say much about his daughter's life and character, but was merely asked to tell the facts about finding her body.

The most important piece of evidence was a letter which was delivered to Providence House on 31st May 1902. The postman who delivered it was to become a witness at the trial. He said it was delivered at the house between three o'clock and fifteen minutes past the hour. From this postmark, which was 'Yoxford:A: May 31, 1902', he concluded it had been posted (if posted in Peasenhall) between half-past six on the Friday night and five minutes to eleven on the Saturday morning, the Saturday being 31st May.

It was addressed: 'Miss Harsent, Providence House, Peasenhall, Saxmundham.' The postman further said that he had delivered three or four other letters to Rose, enclosed in similar envelopes at different times prior to this date. The letter was unsigned. It read:

'D.R.,
      I will try to see you tonight at twelve o'clock at your place if you put a light in your window at ten o'clock for about ten minutes then you can take it out again, don't have a light in your room at twelve I will come round to the back.'

This undoubtedly shed some light on the character of the girl. She was evidently in the habit of receiving a visitor late at night, and we have already seen that access to her room could be gained by a separate staircase, so that other occupants of the house would be quite unaware of such happenings.

This fatal night was curiously appropriate for such a crime. The weather had been sultry, and it was obvious that a storm was brewing. It was to prove one of the worst storms in living memory. Although there was much rumbling of thunder, the storm did not break until late in the evening. A bricklayer, Harry Burgess, was going home, and as he passed the little alley at the entrance to where Gardiner's cottage was situated, he saw him standing at the door. Burgess also recalled that he saw a light high up just below the gable of Providence House. That was, he said, at about five minutes past ten. At the time he thought little of it.

Mrs Dickinson, who kept the little shop next door to the Gardiners, was very nervous of thunder. This was known to Mrs Gardiner, and at about eleven o'clock she went to see if Mrs Dickinson was allright. At the trial, however, these times were extremely hazy.

It was the same with Mrs Crisp, Rose's employer. She was to give evidence in some detail, but for some reason Mr Crisp, who was deaf, was not called at the trial. It appeared that Mrs Crisp went to bed about a quarter past ten that night. When the rain began to pour she awoke. She got up and looked at the window. She also went downstairs and looked around, there was a door open between the dining-room and the kitchen and she shut it. It was very dark in the kitchen itself. Later on, she said, she heard a thud downstairs and a slight scream, but she did not go to investigate. As to the time she contradicted herself and was extremely vague. One would have thought it was extremely callous to hear a scream in her own house and do nothing about it. Actually, the bedroom in which Rose slept was immediately above that occupied by Mr and Mrs Crisp.

In due time the storm passed. At about five o'clock on the Sunday morning, a gamekeeper, James Morris, was walking along the quiet village street. He noticed in the mud caused by the rain, some footprints. These, he declared, led from Gardiner's cottage and went across to Providence House. He described them as representing india-rubber shoes with bars across.

Herbert Stammers, a neighbour of Gardiner's, had also seen something suspicious. He stated the time as about half-past seven on the Sunday morning. He lived in a cottage which overlooked that of Gardiner's. He saw Gardiner making his way to the wash-house in the yard where a large fire was burning. This was unusual at such an hour on a Sunday morning. At the trial a suggestion was made that Gardiner was then burning bloodstained clothes. When the footprints were seen and the wash-house fire, no one then knew that Rose Harsent was dead.

The discovery of Rose's death was made, as the *East Anglian Daily Times* was to announce in its Tuesday issue, by her father. William Harsent was in the habit of going to see his daughter each Sunday morning. Her mother did the girl's washing and her father took her a change of linen early on the Sunday so that she could wear clean clothes.

He went round to the back door, as usual, which he found open. This was unusual as Rose was wont to come down and open it for him. He walked in, to pause horror stricken at the sight that met his eyes. Rose was lying on the kitchen floor, not far from the bottom of the stairs. She was dressed in nightdress and stockings, the nightdress having been burned on each side. Her throat had been cut and there was much blood. He stood for a moment dumbfounded, then he satisfied himself his daughter was dead, covered the body with a rug and went for the local policeman.

The village policeman was a certain Eli Nunn and when he arrived took careful note of what he saw. The girl was lying on her back at the foot of the stairs with her feet to the outer door. He noticed that a bracket on the wall of the staircase supporting a shelf, had been broken. The nightdress was badly burned, the right side and arm of the girl was burnt also, as was the table cloth. Under her head was the charred remains of the *East Anglian Daily Times* of Friday 30th May. This paper was on the floor, behind the neck and shoulders of the girl, but her hair was not burned. He stated her throat was cut from ear to ear and there was much blood in the room. Asked if there were any traces of footprints in the blood, he agreed there were none. There was a smell of paraffin and nearby was a broken lamp. There was also a bottle, smashed to pieces, with the cork still in the neck. The label bore these words, 'Two or three teaspoonfuls, a sixth part to be taken every four hours — Mrs Gardiner's children.'

There was one other unusual feature, fastened to the window, as if to prevent anyone looking in, was a woollen shawl (this proved to be the property of Mrs Crisp). It was fastened to the window-frame by a fork.

Nunn now made his way to the victim's bedroom. There he found the letter of assignation already quoted, also two letters from Gardiner. There were also a number of letters from relatives and friends, together with a bundle of indecent letters, some of them containing verses of a shocking kind. These reflected on the character of Rose Harsent in that she kept them. The writer was traced, a certain Frederick Davis, a youth in the village who was made short work of by Ernest Wild, Gardiner's counsel. Her bed had not been slept in.

It was first thought that Rose had committed suicide, but this was a rather curious conclusion, since the implement could not be found and she had two fatal wounds. It was then surmised she had fallen downstairs and accidentally cut her throat on the lamp glass of the small lamp. But it was discovered that the position of the body ruled out this theory.

The inquest was opened on Tuesday 3rd June in the biggest room in the "Swan". A Mr Chaston was the coroner, and Captain E. B. Levett Scrivener, a local magistrate, was foreman of the jury. It was adjourned while Dr Lay, the local doctor, and Dr Ryder Richardson carried out a post-mortem examination. They soon disposed of the suicide theory, but they discovered she was six months in pregnancy. Meanwhile, on the very day of the opening of the inquest, William Gardiner had been arrested. The inquest was again adjourned.

Gardiner who had been lodged in Ipswich prison, was taken before three magistrates at Saxmundham. The three were all well known local gentry, Mr J. K. Brooke of Sibton, Colonel Abdy Collins and Mr H. M. Doughty of Theberton. A Mr Ridley represented the Crown and a Mr Leighton was for the accused. He was to prove a doughty fighter. Eventually, the jury brought in a unanimous verdict of wilful murder against Gardiner. Three days later he was again before the magistrates, who this time were Mr J. K. Brooke, Mr D. Parry Crooke, Lieutenant Colonel Abdy Collins and Captain Price, R.N.

Gardiner had been brought from Ipswich by an early-morning train and lodged in the Saxmundham police station. The narrow streets of that little town were crowded. Numbers of people had assembled in the hope of seeing him as he was taken to the court, but he was smuggled in by a side entrance. He was committed for trial on 3rd July but it was 7th November before the case actually started. The proceedings were fully reported in the *East Anglian Daily Times*.

The trial took place in the County Hall, Ipswich, the building today as it was then. The Counsel for the Crown was Henry Dickens, sixth son of the famous Victorian novelist, Charles Dickens; while the Counsel for the defence was a comparatively unknown and young man, Mr Ernest Wild. This trial was to be rather momentous for Wild, as it was to make his reputation. The judge was Sir William Grantham, who had been a Conservative M.P. and was known as a political judge. He was something of a character, had the most furious prejudices, and was decidedly biased against Gardiner. Once again extraordinary happenings had been taking place, which would raise a storm of protest to-day.

'No doubt', Sir William Grantham said, 'the prisoner Gardiner has been kept waiting a long time. But you know what has happened. I think I am right in saying that at Yarmouth there is a waxworks exhibition in which there is a representation of the prisoner in the position in which he is supposed to have committed the crime. What does that indicate? Why, that public feeling has been very strong on the subject, and the man now has a much better chance of having ample justice done to him than if he had been tried at the time.'

Ernest Wild found easy prey when he examined George Wright, a country lad against an up-and-coming lawyer, and one wonders if that sort of thing is really justice.

'How much do you earn at Smyth's works?'

'Twelve shillings a week.'

'And Mr Gardiner was your foreman?'

'Yes.'

'What were you doing there [at the Doctor's Chapel] —loitering about to hear what you could?'

'Not exactly that.'

'You thought "there's something to be seen". You were suspicious.'

'Yes.'

'You hoped you would see something done?'

'No.'

'To hear what was going on inside. You thought something wrong was going on?'

'Yes.'

'That is what you went to hear?'

'Yes.'

'That is what you *hoped* to hear?'

'We did not hope anything at all.'

'Is this the first time you have played the eavesdropper?'

'Yes, sir.'

'Let me remind you. Don't you remember a few years ago there was a young man named Ernest Cady, who was going to be married to a young woman? Did you say then you saw him go into an orchard and behave improperly?'

'No, sir.'

'Did you see him go into the orchard?'

'Yes, sir.'

'Did you climb up a tree?'

'I was collecting apples at the time.'

'Did you spread a scandal about those two people then?'

'No, we mentioned it, but we did not mention any scandal about it.'

'Did Cady come and ask you what you meant?'

'Yes,' admitted Wright, 'Cady's mother did.'

'I put it to you, that is the way you and Skinner go about, trying to find out any filth you can.'

Rose Harsent's brother Harry, stated as a witness, that he delivered a copy of the *East Anglian Daily Times* to Gardiner each day. He also confirmed that he had been the bearer of letters between Gardiner and his sister.

The court was then adjourned. It is interesting to note that Mr Dickens stayed at the Great White Horse, Ipswich, the very place made famous by his father in *Pickwick Papers*, with the episode of the lady with the curl papers, being so rudely disturbed by Mr Pickwick.

The next day produced the evidence of a Mr J. S. Richards, secretary at the drill works. He testified that the envelope containing the letter of assignation was the same kind as those used by the firm, to which Gardiner would have had access. They were used by the firm mainly for sending out bills and advertising circulars.

On the Saturday morning, according to the local paper, 'the fair sex was again extensively represented in court, and most of the females present had secured front places in the assembly — a fact which evoked much surprise.'

Gardiner in the witness box explained his presence in Doctor's Chapel as being occasioned by him going up the hill to water his master's horses, and Rose was on her way home after cleaning the chapel. She called him in because she had difficulty in locking the door, and asked if he could help her to get the key moving in a stiff lock.

At the end of the day, Mr W. E. Croft, foreman of the jury,

said to the judge: 'I hope you will allow us to leave Ipswich tonight and send us down to Felixstowe for a change.'

The judge replied: 'There is difficulty about going there tonight. You can go there tomorrow.'

In all probability the jury would have been taken to Felixstowe and returned to Ipswich, in one of those old horse-brakes. On the Monday morning, Mr Justice Grantham spoke to them, 'I am very glad that you were able to go to Felixstowe yesterday, and I hope that you benefitted as well as could be expected.'

'We were well treated,' said the foreman.

(Felixstowe was also represented by the evidence given by Dr W. A. Elliston, who expressed the opinion that there must have been much spurting of blood from the wounds. There is a tablet to his memory in the Parish Church there.)

It was now found necessary to collect a letter from Peasenhall, that had been written by Gardiner. Peasenhall is some twenty-seven miles away. A note was therefore sent to Mr A. F. Garnham, of a garage in the Woodbridge Road, excusing him from exceeding the speed limits. According to the *East Anglian Daily Times*, he did nobly. The journey there and back to Ipswich was made in under three hours. This speed was made possible by a tacit understanding that no penalties should attach to the violation of the law as to speed of motor cars. Remember this was in 1902.

The judge's summing up was extremely biased, and at a quarter past four on the Monday afternoon the jury retired. At half-past six the judge came back: 'I understand', he said to the foreman, 'you want to ask a few questions?' The question concerned the absence of the blood-stained clothes. It was nearly half past eight before the jury returned again. When asked if they were agreed, it was stated that one was not in agreement. Asked if there was any chance of an agreement, the answer was "No". This staunch East Anglian caused a second trial.

The next morning the London papers had taken up the

case, and even *The Times* allowed Mrs Gardiner to state her case and appeal for funds through its columns. She was so far successful, but the sum contributed was not stated.

The second trial opened on 21st January 1903, and was again held at the County Hall. Mr Henry Dickens still represented the Crown, and Mr Ernest Wild was for the defence. But the judge was different, this time Mr Justice Lawrence took the place of Sir William Grantham. Ernest Wild rather bullied P. C. Nunn, but he was checked by the judge, who thought his action was unfair.

The evidence proceeded on the same lines as before, with the significant exception that no less than three different attempts at confession had been made. One of these was taken from a tramp, written at some length and with complete illiteracy. They were dismissed, as these occasions foster such things. Also in trying to determine if Gardiner had tried to destroy any of his clothes, there was a good deal of wrangling as to how many shirts he possessed. He professed to only two, one on and one off, neither could he be moved from the point. His wife stuck to the fact. Also the question of handwriting in the letter of assignation was again brought to the front, and the evidence of the experts was somewhat discredited.

It was five o'clock when the jury retired, but it was not until nearly a quarter past seven before they returned. 'Are you agreed upon the verdict?' asked the clerk.

The sensation in court at the answer could only be imagined, 'No, sir', said the foreman. The judge was as astonished as anyone else. 'You are not agreed? Is there any chance of your agreeing?'

'No, sir', replied the foreman.

'None whatever?'

'I am afraid not.' The jury was therefore dismissed.

But the curious fact emerged that whereas at the first trial only one man disagreed about Gardiner's guilt, now only one was against his innocence. The number was reversed.

Once again crowds thronged the streets and the offices of

the *East Anglian Daily Times* were besieged for the full report that was to appear in the evening paper.

Gardiner still remained in prison. He was to have come up for trial at Bury St Edmunds. However, on 29th January, five days after the second trial, the Crown decided to go no further and Gardiner was released.

He left Peasenhall, which was far too unhealthy for him, shaved off his beard and went to London, either to work in a small business or to take one of his own. He was seen later by more than one person, including Dr Ryder Richardson who had dispelled the suicide theory and pointed to the evidence of murder. What became of Gardiner no one knows, he may have changed his name although it was suggested he emigrated to Canada and his identity completely lost. It was always firmly believed in the village that he was guilty.

Meanwhile in Peasenhall churchyard there is a well tended grave, which bears the inscription: 'In Affectionate Remembrance of Rose Anne Harsent whose life was cruelly taken on the 1st of June, 1902 in her 23rd year.'

I have recently had a letter from an admirer in South Africa who asserts that it was a Mr James Hunt who had a boot and shoe business in Woodbridge who was the dissenting juror which resulted in the retrial of Gardiner and his subsequent acquittal.

10

EXTRACTS FROM POSTAL RECORDS

I have heard Will Honeycomb say, A Woman seldom Writes her
mind but in her Postscript.   Sir Richard Steele

I have been loaned a Post Office Record Book of Saxmundham and District, covering the years 1862 when my
mother was a "mawther", to 1906. Unfortunately some of the
earlier pages have been cut away, which might have yielded
even more memories. However, we must be thankful for what
remains, and which gives such a wonderful view into the past,
when my grandmother was writing to her gals away in London
and when individuality loomed large.

There are two lists of village offices, giving the names of the
postmasters or mistresses, whereas later lists merely name the
villages. These were made for the quarterly payments. The
one for 1862 merely gives the initials, that for 1863 the
Christian names. And we should recall that some of these held
the office for very long periods, passing it on to succeeding
generations. Here follows the list:

Yoxford, Mrs Hall
Peasenhall, Emma Freeman
Heveningham, John Fisk
Westleton, Walter Salter
Middleton, Joseph Broom
Darsham, William Etheridge
Bramfield, Benjamin Cattermole
Knodishall, Samuel Smith
Leiston, Susan Smith
Aldbro', Horatio Salter

Benhall, Isaac Batho
Friston, W. J. B. Gildersleeves
Snape, Isaac Kerridge
Rendham, John Andrews
Badingham, Robert Foulsham Gissing
Theberton, William Tongate
Kelsale, Robert Aldous

Some of these received as little as £3 p.a., some £4, others £6 (including Mr Broom of Middleton), while others soared as high as £10, £11, £12, £13, Leiston £26 and Aldeburgh heading the list with £27.

The daily mail to Leiston and Aldeburgh commenced on 1st December 1862; and of course the mail to Leiston would have been considerable because of Garrett's Works. These call to mind the old mailcarts that are listed in the directories, making their way to Saxmundham, hail, rain or shine.

Now comes a list of the numbers of letters sent out for one week in 1863 for delivery to the undermentioned places: Aldeburgh 2,286, Leiston 1,517, Yoxford 1,753, Friston 761, Middleton 487, Bramfield 269, Darsham 246. This is followed by a note that Hyde & Co., Sealing Wax Manufacturers, Fleet Street, supply it for 23s. per cwt; and John and Edward Wright, Twine Manufacturers Universal Works, Milwall, Poplar at 9s.6d. a dozen lb; this would have been in balls.

On 27th February 1863 four packets of green tape were received, the same again on 23rd September. But on 14th March 1864 they had twenty packets, on 26th October 1865, twenty-five packets, and on 4th July 1867 another twenty-five.

Some of the large houses and sundry persons had their own postal bags, evidently collected by the mail cart. For this privilege they paid £1, 21s., and even £5 a year at Michaelmas. On 1st June 1864 C. M. Doughty commenced a letter bag at Theberton Hall. He was the author of the famous *Arabia Deserta*, at first despised, now ranged as a classic piece of work done at his life's risk.

The list of complaints received contain several items of interest, since such were to be had in those days.

1863. Reg. No 67121. Letter Posted at Saxmundham by Rev Hollond, Benhall, 3rd December, addressed Ed. Laporett, 133 Upper Thames Street. The letter was purloined by a boy in Mr Laporett's office. (Contained a cheque for £18 payable to bearer.)

14th December. Reg. No 92023. Letter stated to be posted in London addressed to Mr Owles, Leiston, containing half soverign.

15th December. Reg. No 91133. Letter delivered to wrong person addressed to Miss Dowsing, Saxmundham, containing 6s. worth of stamps. Stamps returned to Secretary's Office 22nd December.

25th March, 1863 enquiry made by Miss Cavell, Leiston, about a newspaper taxed 2d., over 4oz. Reg. No 22656. [She would have been of the same family as Nurse Cavell.]

17th October, Letter enquired for by Mr Kersey, Knodishall. Posted at Leiston directed to Mrs Kersey, [c/o] Mr Lincoln, Aldboro', contents a photograph and letter; the letter afterwards found by Mr Kersey in his own house.

29th November 1864, Enquiry for a letter posted at Bath addressed to Miss Osborne, Kent House, Aldeburgh, Suffolk, containing a piece of [bride cake]. Not recollected in this office. [Do you remember when they used to say — 'I don't fare to recollect'?]

It is not without interest to note the large number of registered letters handled in so sparsely populated an area, as it was in those years. For example, in 1905 those containing money or stamps, known as remittance letters, amounted to 5,149 — a clear reminder that only the very few had cheque books.

There was also a notice kept of the number of circulars received, such as *Mother Seigal's Syrup*; easily number one in quantity. *Dr Dodd's Kidney Pills, Dr William's Pink Pills*; recalling that patent medicines flourished in country districts. Then there were *Dr Tibble's Vi Cocoa, Mazawattee Tea* (not forgetting the picture of grandmother enjoying a cup, with a granddaughter by her side); and not least, *Mrs Welldon's Journal*.

And so we might let the old book lie, with its record of letters delivered week by week, numbers of railway borne parcels, forms received and instructions noted which call to mind the little old country post offices, smelling of sugar and spice and all things nice; not forgetting the bottles of medicine waiting to be called for. Neither should we let the memory fade of the poor old postmen, trudging many a weary mile by gritty roads or well worn footpaths now covered over by weeds or ploughed out of existence. They were always a welcome visitor to many a cottage or farmhouse door. Always cheery, sunshine or rain, from Michaelmas to Michaelmas, perhaps to be rewarded with a cup of tea or even a mug of small beer. Those old fellows seemed to know from whence the letters came and the senders. 'Thare yew are tewgether, another from yare Eliza. I hoop she git along well. Nice gal she were to be sure.' Remember also that the famous Victorian Postmaster General, the Rt Hon. Henry Fawcett, married the daughter of the litigious old notoriety, Newson Garrett of Aldeburgh.

Of course some of those old letter carriers might have complained. 'There's too many Rivetts in this place. I can't fare to track 'em down. Less see, there's Paddy Rivett, Friday Rivett, Saturday Rivett, Happy Rivett, Poop's Rivett and Dutch Rivett!' He might have said the same about the Barham family.

And here follows a letter that must have passed through the old post office at that time, carried by a penny stamp. It is from my grandmother to one of her gals:

Rackford Farm

'My dear Daughter,

Many many thanks for the things you so kindly sent this morning. How kind and good of you. You should have seen us blaring [crying] over against the other-mother, father. Soon opened the box, I to the letter. They were soon scattered on the breakfast table. Well, I just managed a soaked rust for my breakfast, but can't manage much at breakfast. Well, I can't tell you this time how I like them, as must answer to say I got it safely, also the letter Sunday morning, but thought about the posting of it. . . .

Oh yes, there have been a good many goodbyes, but God gave me strength, and I commit them, or you all, to the fatherly care, as at first. One verse helped me "Be strong and of a good courage, I will be with thee." I opened on it, you will find it in Joshua, 1st chapter 5.7.9.verse.

Yes, dear, I shall have to brew soon, if I am spared. I wished you could have had some beer, but no chance in London. I am glad you enjoyed what we sent, but not baking today. I will write to Susie if I am spared. My love to her. . . .

I hope you got my letter about a fortnight ago, little over. Ethel directed it for me, and I sent it by the baker lad who calls from Leiston, as I have my bread of him. Asked him if he was going to Broom's, he said "Yes". I asked him if he would put it in the post for me. I was only afraid he forgot it as he put it in his pocket, as I put three stamps in, I think.

I was glad you got to Lie's [my mother's] the day after Xmas. I should a liked to have joined you, but I was otherwise engaged. I did think of you.

Well, Susie, the old year is gone, and I do hope this one we are just entered upon may be the best we ever lived. I feel my time is getting short, it is like a mile stone, one mile the less. Of course it is to us all, but especially to me.

Betsy Newson is dead and buried since I last wrote, so God keep taking one here, one there. Well, thank God, we are all spared, hope we shall be a few years.'

It was claimed that one of the sons of Childs and Son, the well known printers of Bungay invented the method of perforating postage stamps. Previously, stamps were thick and had to be clipped off, the word "paid" written on the letter and a penny paid over the counter when posting it.

11

A SUFFOLK YEOMAN'S HOME

Stay, stay at home, my heart, and rest;
Home-keeping hearts are happiest.
Longfellow

Before Constable noticed the beauty of a Suffolk sky, there were artists in every builder's yard in the county, when Elizabeth I was Queen, and they were local artists at that. Their creations were all the more satisfying because they were spontaneous. If they had only local materials to deal with, there must have been an inspiration that ran through all their work. If a sculptor could see an angel in a block of marble, they could see a home in a bit of clay and the oak tree that grew out of it, at a time when every man was his own architect.

Ruskin in "The Lamp of Life" section of *The Seven Lamps of Architecture* said: 'I believe the right question to ask, respecting all ornaments, is simply this: 'Was it done with enjoyment — was the carver happy while he was about it?' If we alter "carver" to builder, where an old Suffolk home is concerned, the answer must be yes.

The one grudge I have against our Victorian ancestors is they let so much of beauty go, even aggressively destroying their own inheritance, rather than preserve it. It is good to realize that more respect is being given today to old buildings, rather than allow them to be blasted into rubble.

For example I wonder how much this old house would fetch today, if it was still standing? The amount would have "whooly stammed" my old grandfather, if he could have known about it. But alas, it has gone the way of all flesh.

It is an early photograph which I found when I was rummaging through an old book shop, and judging by the hats of the boys would be about the seventies of last century. I also think the woman carrying the pail of water from the pond or well, and the man in shirt sleeves, sitting sideways on a really nice antique chair, are posing for the picture. But what a delightful scene it is, perhaps of farmhouse down-scaled into cottage in the days of a great peace and flower-scented air.

I think it must have been a farmhouse by reason of the outbuildings and the horse harrows left just in that untidy fashion after use, which too often characterized agricultural life and habits in those days.

In any case it is a real Suffolk homestead with its shingle-tiled roof that creeples so gently, and had stood so many summers and winters. True, it is going at the eaves a bit, possibly because the landlord "'ont do a thing" to the old place. But how beautiful are those two dormers with latticed windows. What snug rooms they must have been as the dawn came for another morning. Long years before, the two lower windows would have been glazed in the same way, but they have been modernized into nice little square panes. But do not miss the little bracket over the door as also the drip-board over the further window. And I rather surmise the thatch portion of the lean-to at the far end was the dairy.

The old farmer taking his ease in the sun, is at the business end of the house because it was there the baking, cooking, washing and brewing were done. This is apparent by the chimney stack, as also that little extension which was an old brick oven. What pleasant smells and lovely tasting food came out from thence at least once a week.

Those "warmints o' boys" do not seem to be having too bad a time, although it is on record that boys were treated rough in those early days. They might have been giving a hand with carrying the water up the steps. In any case they are not up to mischief, otherwise they would have got out of the reach of the old man's stick. In fact they do not seem to mind him a bit so he could not have been a bad sort.

A note on the back of the picture states that it is a cottage at Capel since destroyed, but as there are two Capels miles apart from one another, and as I do not know which is the one here shown, I will tell a little about each as described in the 1879 directory.

Capel St Andrew is a village on Butley Water, four miles west of Orford and has no church. The population in 1871 was 209. However, Alfred Chambers was a coprolite raiser, Samuel Pratt was a carpenter; both Mrs Christopher Clodd and Mrs Mary Ann Stebbings were farmers and four other men farmers made the list. That leaves 201 people unaccounted for.

Capel St Mary, named from an ancient chapel, was on the old Hadleigh branch line and even had a station master all to itself. It was also one of Suffolk's rich livings, with a population in 1871 of 593. William Beer was a cattle dealer, farmer and butcher; John Goodchild was a farmer and carman. James Worsley, a farmer and veterinary surgeon, lived at the Manor House. Henry Potts was a beer retailer and jobber (whatever that meant), George Underwood was a wheelwright, Abraham Cole was a seed grower, while James Cole was a thrashing machinist. There were five other farmers, two shoemakers, a tailor, carpenter, blacksmith; and two shopkeepers. Also Levi Skitter, who might have come out of the Bible, combined the offices of harness maker with that of rate collector. So I do not think he could have been all that popular.

To complete the picture, Stephen Scarfe was a miller, coal and manure agent. But that might have been a water mill because the village was 'situated in the vale of a small stream falling into the Stour'. Here then, with a parish clerk named John Gull, you have a tight little community that might be described as self-contained. Moreover, it was in all probability on the route of the Romans when they came into the country of the South Folk.

12

RAMBLES THROUGH AN OLD SUFFOLK DIRECTORY

> In this catalogue of *books which are no books—biblia a-biblia*—I reckon Court Calendars, Directories, Pocket-Books, Draught Boards bound and lettered at the back, Scientific Treatises, Almanacs, Statutes at Large.
>
> Charles Lamb

In spite of the above quotation, I do not know of anything more pleasant than turning over the pages of an old directory of Suffolk, compiled before life became so harassing and troublesome. Come then and join me in a hunt through the pages of a Victorian Kelly's *Directory* for 1879. We will begin with the pubs.

First, it must be remembered that most village inns were waymarks. If asking the way you were not guided from church to church; and if it was a question of travelling a horse, as the old grooms used to do, the direction would be, say, from Kirton "Greyhound" (known as the "Dog"), to Martlesham "Lion", thence to the "Queen's Head" at Woodbridge, Saxmundham "Bell" to the Crown Inn at Framlingham. The inn yards would be wide open, there would be a bell labelled "Ostler", and probably a sign saying it was a Posting House, not, of course, for letters but for a horse to take you on to the next stop.

Also you could get a bed and breakfast fit for a countryman, for a small sum that almost escapes the eyes in these days of inflation; and a drop of beer that would vary in glory from one house to another. No indications of good eating, or *cordon bleu* cooking, because they had never "heerd o' sich a thing"; and the good wife knew what she was doing.

The names of these inns are most intriguing, and in some cases quite misleading. For example if you came across the "Racehorse", you naturally expect to find it under Newmarket. But nothing of the kind, it was in an out of the way village of Westhall, remote from any gallops.

For convenience sake we might classify these houses into sections, and the chief industry in Suffolk in those times was that of agriculture. So here we go. There was one "Cow and Gate" and one "Cow and Pail", one "Harrow", one "Jolly Farmer" (which they seldom were), one "Lamb", which may have been ecclesiastical; one "Plough and Fleece", four "Fleeces", and one "Plough and Sail", which still has open doors at Snape. Then come five "Rams", three "Shepherd and Dogs", one "Sedge Sheaf" which is naturally in the Brecklands at Lakenheath, only one "Sickle", one "Bushel", two "Mills", one "Spotted Cow", one "Waggon", four "Waggon and Horses", two "Wheatsheafs" and four "Woolpacks". To which might be added one only "Village Maid" and nineteen "Bulls".

We might now turn to the countryman's national drink, *viz* beer. So there were two "Barley Mows", two "Bottles", two "Brewers", one "Malt and Hops", two "Brewers Arms", one "Hop Pole", two "Tankards", one "John Barleycorn" and eleven "Tuns".

Now to sport, with one "Bowling Green", one "Bull and Dog", an old and beastly sport; two "Cricketers", five "Dog and Partridges", eight "Falcons", a very old sport; and two "Hawks". Fifteen "Foxes", one "Fox and Ball", a curious combination; one "Fox and Goose" and nine "Fox and Hounds". Then comes one "French Horn" to sound Tally-ho, and twenty-one "Greyhounds", complete with one "Gun". In this section we must include one "Hare", six "Hare and Hounds", and one "Hound". Now follows two "Huntsmen and Hounds", and one "Sportsman"; and "Old Fox", one "Running Buck", three

"Bucks" and three "Buck's Heads".

We could now have a look at horses and find there were five "Black Horses", one "Chestnut Horse", four "Coach and Horses", one "Horse and Groom", one "Rampant Horse" (although this really belongs to Kent), three "Sorrel Horses", no less than eight "Horseshoes"; and to complete the picture, one "Tally Ho". Not forgetting "The Great White Horse" that is at Ipswich, and the lady with the curl papers.

Now follow the various beasts, the replicas of which appear in the old churches from the bestiaries, sometimes visible on the pew-ends. They came to life from tales told by old sailors home from the sea, illuminated by rum and imagination. Two "Bears" appear, one "Bear and Bells", one "Black Lion", and two "Blue Boars." Now follow three "George and Dragons", four "Green Dragons", two "Elephant and Castles". There were three "Golden Lions", four "Griffins", well known from church parapets; and one "Jolly Tiger" (with the lady inside her). However, there was only one "Leopard", but there were twelve "Lions" and no less than twenty-one "Red Lions". Now follows one "Tiger's Head", with one "Turk's Head", two "Unicorns", one "Golden Boar", one "White Bear", one "White Horse" and one "White Lion".

This leads us naturally to birds, one "Bird-in-Hand", one "Blackbird", one "Black Eagle", one "Blue Swan", thirteen "Cocks", one "Cock and Bell", one "Cock and Magpie", one "Cock and Pye" and one "Cock's Head". Then we have one "Eagle", one "Eagle and Rising Sun", one "Four Swans", no less than thirty-six "Swans", one "Three Swans". Now come two "Hawks", three "Magpies", one "Ostrich", one "Parrot And Punch Bowl", near the sea, three "Spread Eagles", one "White Swan" and one "Dove".

There are not many in the fish line, with one "Butt and Oyster", butt being a small flat fish; two "Dolphins", one "Oyster" and three "Pickerels". We might end this section with one "Fishing Buss", one "Herring Fishery", one "Three Herrings" and one "Safe Harbour". But we must not omit one

"Sea Horse", three "Compasses", nine "Anchors" and one "Blue Anchor".

We might continue with shipping, one "Neptune", five "Ships", one "Ship Launch", one "Shipwright's Arms", one "Three Mariners", one "Steam Packet", one "Pilot", one "Boat" and one "Barge", one "Mariner's Arms", one "Welcome Sailor", one "Happy Return", and one "Sailor's Home". Concluding with three "Lifeboat's", and one "Jolly Sailor", asking the question as to why sailors were always jolly?

Royalty provide a large array with thirty-six "Crowns", five "Crown and Anchors", one "Crown and Castle", one "Duke of Edinburgh", one "Duke of Kent", one "Duke of York" (who marched his men about); two "Duke's Heads", one "Emperor", nine "Georges", one "Royal George", one "King of Prussia". Now come ten "King's Arms", thirty-one "King's Heads", three "Victorias", and one "Maid's Head", presumably Elizabeth I, our Queen; and two "Castles". Then there were five "Prince of Wales", one "Queen's Arms", twenty-nine "Queen's Heads", three "Royal Williams", one "Rose and Crown", one "Three Crowns", relative to the county's coat of arms; one "Three Kings", one "Windsor Castle" and one "Royal Oak".

These might be followed by the nobility, with two "Dukes of Marlborough", one "Marlborough Head", two "Wellingtons", one "Duke of Wellington", one "Marquis of Granby", four "Marquis of Cornwallis", and one "Grafton Arms".

The Church comes next, with eighteen "Angels", and one "Old Angel", which must refer to the building rather than the heavenly orders. No less than thirty-two "Bells", one "Black Bell", three "Eight Bells", six "Five Bells", one "Six Bells", two "Ten Bells", one "One Bell" and one "Old Bell". One "Christopher" (to be found on the walls of old churches as the patron saint of travellers), two "Cross Inns", five "Cross Keys", the sign of "St Peter", one "Golden Fleece", one "St Edmund's Head" and one "Salutation".

In the old days the section under "Trades" seemed to comprise everything. For example, my great grandfather was a surgeon and he appears in the Lincolnshire *Directory* three times; once as a tradesman, once as a surgeon and again under the gentry. Another most interesting thing is the number of trades that have ceased to exist. If you ask the average person today what a fellmonger was, he or she will look in blank astonishment and remark to never having heard of such an occupation. I have been intrigued by the one and only case, practising a lonely but probably lucrative business of dealing in skins. I have also been intrigued by industries that belong to some counties and not to others. This list is in alphabetical order and is not without interest.

First comes an Accoucheur, who hails from Orford. This was also the accomplishment of a doctor, but more often than not by the village woman or the midwife; the vicar's wife acting as a locum.

Now comes the Agricultural Machine Makers and Agents. Suffolk was noted for these, the chief iron industry in the country. Foundery Road, Ipswich is its memorial. There were more than one would think. They are accompanied by Agricultural Machine Owners, of which there were a number, making a living letting out engines to those who could not afford to buy them.

Ale and Porter Merchants and Agents come next. I must confess to never having investigated the mysteries of Porter — shades of Sarah Gamp. Presumably it is marketed under some fancy name today.

Now comes a name I always like to see, *viz.* Appraiser. Its derivation is the word praise. This is followed by Artists, and I was surprised to note that John Duval, who illustrated the first Stud Book; and both E. R. and T. Smythe are in the list. They do it a bit different today.

There were Asphalters and Asphalters Merchants, followed by quite a different line of business — Assayers who dealt in bullion, metals and minerals, and were metallurgical chemists and platinum manufacturers.

There was only one Bacon Dealer, but four Bacon and Ham Curers. Bakers were numerous in spite of the fact that many folks baked their own bread. And there was one Muffin Baker. Bakers always claimed to be Pastry-cooks and Confectioners. At least on their paper bags and windows.

The muffin man called to mind my boyhood days, when he made his rounds in the evening. You heard his bell in the distance, coming nearer and nearer. It was rather like Leerie's Lamplighter: 'For every night at tea-time and before you take your seat, . . . he comes posting up the street.' His bell was the only sound that heralded his approach.

This is followed by the Baking Powder Manufacturers, shades of the old cooks who used plain flour, before the self-raising variety came on the market. Then three Barge Builders, with a couple of Barge Owners. The next is interesting because he was a Bark Merchant of Wangford and Wrentham. Reminiscent of when they barked the trees with special tools to provide tanning for leather. He is automatically followed by Curriers and Leather Sellers, Fellmongers, etc, Basket and Sieve Makers come next, then so much in use. This was a very old industry based on the growing of osiers.

There are not many Bathing Machine Proprietors, but those old contraptions on huge wheels could be pulled down to the water's edge to enable bathers to get into the water unseen, although the bathing costumes in those days were more extensive in coverage than hot pants are today. Bikinis would have been shrieked at.

Strangely enough there were only two Bed and Mattress Manufacturers, and they were both at Ipswich. Furniture Brokers and Dealers took the place of House Furnishers; with one Chair Maker, who worked at Aspall. There was also a Cornice Maker, Horsehair Seating Manufacturer, Feather Dresser, which may have applied to feather beds. But a Plumassier was one who dealt in plumes, so this trade might have belonged to those awful funerals with weepers.

Beer retailers appear in large numbers, followed by Beer Fittings Manufacturers. With them we might include Cork Cutters and Manufacturers; and of course, Coopers.

Berlin Wool Repositories, with whom we might include Fancy Repositories, which were usually run by little old ladies, who always had a job to find what was wanted amongst the mass of papers and cards in her small shop. In those days there was no traffic in get-well cards, but you could buy those dainty valentines and the new Christmas cards that were coming into vogue. Also there were two Bird Dealers, one at Ipswich, the other at Bury, they are now represented by up-and-coming Pet Shops. They are linked up with Bird and Animal Preservers.

Birmingham and Sheffield Warehouses speak for themselves, also Boat Builders and Boat Owners. This was pronounced "bo-at" in old Suffolk. They could hardly have managed without Bolt, Nut and Rivet Manufacturers and the Nail Merchants.

Boot and Shoe Manufacturers were numerous, and there were Boot Upper Manufacturers in those days. But what on earth was a Boot Closer? Grindery Dealers dealt in shoemakers' odds and ends.

There were more brewers about in those days than now, but only one Brewer's Chemist who hailed from Earl Soham. And there were a couple of British Wine Manufacturers, and plenty of Malsters.

Bricklayers were to be had for the asking and a fair number of Brick and Tile Manufacturers, together with Brush and Broom Makers; an interesting craft; also Grainers.

Butchers there were always, together with Butter Merchants, Cheesemongers and Cheese Factors. But the people that intrigue me were the Candle Manufacturers, an interesting industry rather in decline in these days, but highly suggestive of "The Land of Nod".

> All by myself I have to go,
> With none to tell me what to do —

All alone beside the streams
And up the mountain-sides of dreams.

The old farmhouses used to make their own candles.

There was only one Cane Worker, a number of Carmen, also Coach and Carriage builders and Cart and Van Builders. Also Coach Body Makers and Coach Painters. It must be remembered that some of those painters turned into artists of no mean school. Then there were Coach Smiths, and one Coach Spring Manufacturer.

But we have overlooked the Cattle Dealers, Cattle Condiment Manufacturers; and one Castrator, who lived at Gislingham. This list might include Horse Breakers (Horse Gentlers at Wickham Market), Horse Clippers and Horse Slaughterers. Then come Horse Collar Manufacturers, Livery Stable Keepers, Saddlers and Harness Makers, and Whip Makers. And one odd Iron Harness Bracket Manufacturer.

We might now include such people as Color Manufacturers, Color Men, a Crayon Maker, Lime Burner, Drysalter, Dyers and Scourers, a Gutta Percha Warehouse, Offal Dealer, Rosin Merchants, Solvent Manufacturer, only one Italian Warehousemen, and a Sash and Cord Line Dealer.

Farmers and Bailiffs take up no less than nineteen pages. To which must be added Hurdle Makers, Rake Makers and Thatchers; and not least Coprolite Raisers. This could almost include Agricultural and Veterinary Chemists.

Naturally there were a lot of Fishermen, Smack Owners, Sail Makers, Mast and Block Makers.

Millers come next, with Millstone Manufacturers, Millwrights and Measure Makers. Those old wooden measures figure as antiques today, at a good price. Then as the Mills always attracted a lot of vermin, we might include Rat and Mouse Trap Manufacturers and Vermin Destroyers.

Well Sinkers and Pump Makers were much in evidence, as also Wheelwrights. But Church Bellhangers must have been a trade on its own, and full of difficulties; together with

Whitesmiths, Locksmiths and Bill Posters.

Mangle Makers sound strange today, but many a poor woman has made a few pence by putting a notice in her window, 'Mangling Done Here'. What horrible old machines they were.

Of metal workers it could include Galvanizers, Iron Bucket Manufacturers and Metal Perforators.

We might end the list with various odds and ends, such as Curiosity Dealers, Marble Chimney Piece Importers, a Lapidary, Flax Merchants, Rope and Twine Manufacturers; not forgetting the old Rope Walks that still exist by name only. Leather Bucket Manufacturers, Lath Renders, Lath Merchants, Hoop Makers, Timber Benders, Higglers (who came to the backdoor with a basket), Gun Flint Manufacturers, Naptha Manufacturers, Trunk and Portmanteau Makers. But what on earth were Sun Burner Manufacturers? We will end with Straw Bonnet and Hat Makers who were all women with one exception.

13

THE ENIGMATIC COLONEL TOMLINE
(1812 – 1889)

It is a pity he couldna be hatched o'er again, an' be hatched
different.   George Eliot

To understand the rather enigmatic Colonel Tomline
(1812–1889) it is necessary to know something of his ancestry.
He came of an ancient and respectable Suffolk family which
had held land in Bacton, Suffolk from the fifteenth century.

His grandfather, George Pretyman was born at Bury St Edmunds on 9th October 1750 and educated at the grammar
school there, and at Pembroke Hall, Cambridge where he
distinguished himself in mathematics, being senior wrangler
and Smith's prizeman in 1772. He graduated as a B.A. that
same year and was appointed fellow and shortly afterwards
tutor of his college in 1773.

On William Pitt being sent to the university at the early age
of fourteen, Pretyman was appointed his tutor, probably on
the recommendation of the Master of Pembroke Hall. Pitt
early developed a close friendship with his tutor, which he
maintained till his death and which established his fortune. In
1775 Pretyman proceeded to an M.A. and was appointed
moderator of the university in 1781.

In January 1787 Pretyman succeeded Thurlow as Bishop of
Lincoln and Dean of St Paul's. It is said that on Pitt's application on behalf of his friend, the king remarked, 'Too
young, too young, can't have it!' but that on the minister
replying that had it not been for Pretyman he would not have

been in office, the King answered, 'He shall have it Pitt! He shall have it!'

In June 1803 the Bishop of Lincoln took the name of Tomline on a considerable estate at Riby, Lincolnshire being left him by the will of Marmaduke Tomline thus becoming George Pretyman Tomline. Between the legator and the legatee there was no relationship and but a slight acquaintance, the bishop not having seen Tomline more than five or six times in his life. In 1820 Tomline was appointed Bishop of Winchester and at the same time vacated the Deanery of St Paul's. In 1823 Tomline established his claim to a Nova Scotia baronetcy, which on the death of Sir Thomas Pretyman in 1749 had been allowed to lapse. Henceforward to the end of his life he was known as Sir George Pretyman Tomline, but his eldest son on succeeding to the estate laid no claim to the honour.

The bishop died on 14th November 1827 and was buried in Winchester near the western end of the south aisle. He married in 1784 Elizabeth the eldest daughter and co-heiress of Thomas Maltby of Germains, Buckinghamshire, a woman of considerable ability and character, who was informal and consulted by her husband on all important matters in which he was engaged. By her the bishop had three sons, William Edward Tomline, M.P. for Truro, George Thomas Pretyman Tomline, Chancellor of Lincoln and Prebendary of Winchester and Richard Pretyman, Tomline Precentor of Lincoln.

The bishop was an anti-Calvinist and was against the Roman Catholic recognition in the repeal of the Test Act.

His successor was William Edward Tomline, M.P., who was the first owner of No 1 Carlton House Terrace, the famous row of houses in the Mall, London, built by Nash. It was let on a crown lease for seventy-five years. In due time the vast estates came to Colonel George Tomline of Orwell Park, Nacton, Suffolk, who was the builder of modern Felixstowe, providing it not only with a railway built over his own land but a dock that was to become known as the "Gateway to Europe".

When he died it was said of him: 'Another of the great figures of our local life has passed away and, in some respects the most remarkable of them all. Great in his talents, great in his wealth, great in his enterprise . . . the ruler over the destinies of so many score of desirable farms, the lord of an army of gamekeepers and dependants, the king in fact of a little principality. . . . He seemed to have a real love of opposition and fighting. In Fact he gave the impression of being a spoilt child.'

A little more light on the youthful George Tomline has been shown by Virginia Surtees in her book *Charlotte Canning*. It would appear that whereas George lived at No 1 Carlton Terrace, No 4 had been let to Lord Stuart of Rothesay, who was at the very desirable post of the Paris Embassy, and that his elder daughter, the Hon. Charlotte Stuart had her eye on the son at number one; and this is what she wrote:

'I hear on every side that Mr Tomline is to be *beaufrère* to me & I at last write to ask, not if it is true, but how much is true. Has he been making up to Lou? [Her sister.] We think it a little suspicious that his name has not even been mentioned in your letter or hers.'

Again, a Lady Granville writing from Paris stated: 'Letters from Rome say Miss Stuart is going to marry Mr Tomline, £25,000 a year, handsome, agreeable, young, but that Lady Betty [her mother] opposes it. It is the girl's doing, but *la Madre* wants rank.'

Tomline did not marry, he entered the Army and became M.P. for Shrewsbury, a constituency he shared with Disraeli, and later he was M.P. for Great Grimsby.

Charlotte became a lady-in-waiting to Queen Victoria and was very intimate with the royal family. She married John Charles Canning who was to become the first Viceroy of India, when the Crown took over after the Mutiny.

She is described in the *Dictionary of National Biography* as a 'noble and singularly gifted woman, who was carried off by jungle fever in the latter part of 1861'.

This raises the rather interesting question: was the Colonel crossed in love, and did this account for his irascible temper?

. Like his grandfather he had an inordinate love of acquiring land. He must have had a vast estate, as he owned land from Nacton to Felixstowe, and would buy up anything that came onto the market. His eyes always seemed to be on the future and he built himself an observatory in the grounds of Orwell Park, which is still in use.

His death came by paralysis, lying there for eight months then in a coma for five days. One of the two doctors who signed the death certificate was Dr William Roche of Berner's Street, Ipswich.

The disposal of his body was kept a strict secret, but it turned out he wished to be cremated, a rather frowned-upon end in those days. The body was taken to No 1 Carlton House Terrace and the service was held at St Martins-in-the-Field (the incumbent being the Reverend John F. Kitto), from thence to the special bay at Waterloo Station for Brookwood, then the only crematorium in England. His funeral was attended by four gentlemen, one of them being his solicitor. He was within the first hundred to be so disposed of, the first cremation in England being in 1882.

He had no family ties and paid no regard to public opinion. It is said that he went on one occasion with a lady friend to hear Spurgeon preach, and was introduced to the great preacher in his vestry. Spurgeon was sitting drinking sherry and asked his visitors to join him.

He was succeeded by Captain Ernest Pretyman.

I think George would give a grunt of satisfaction if he could know what is happening to his Docks now called the Port of Felixstowe. 'European Ferries, which last week won its fight to keep the port of Felixstowe, yesterday unveiled a £350,000 improvement scheme at the docks. The money will pay for new fork-lift trucks to cope with increased roll-on-roll-off traffic and help improve container park facilities.' (*East Anglian Times*, 29th October 1976.)

14

A SPLENDID RECEPTION

Long may they live, and happy may they be,
Blest with content and from misfortune free.

Our Victorian forefathers were only too glad to commemorate great occasions. Such a one is the subject of this splendid photograph, Captain Pretyman's reception in the grounds of Orwell Park, Nacton, soon after his marriage in 1894.

It was a great event for local people whose names were identified in the neighbourhood and a splendid opportunity of getting together. But as far as the present is concerned its chief significance is in the exhibition of fashions, all dated even to the year. Local dress exhibitions at museums could not equal it. As one would suppose the female guests are more fashion conscious than the men. Today, it is difficult to distinguish a grandmother from her daughters, but here for all to see and remember she is self-evident; and by no means seeks to disguise herself as being of the then up-and-coming generation. For example, you know that the lady second left in the front row is a grandmother because of her side curls and her bonnet; and I must say she looks a dear old thing.

But what of the ladies who are not that old, with their leg-of-mutton sleeves, heavily draped figures, and the last word in millinery? They have the air of matriarchs every one. Whereas the matrons are all dressed more or less alike, with bonnets that seem to suggest mourning rather than such a festive occasion; the young women, their daughters, have individual creations, representing hours and hours of stitchwork; and have Bond Street, London, W. as their venue.

As for the men, well, the beards belong to the grandfathers, plus the tall hats, while middle-age adopts the bowler, and youth the dashing boater, which latter today has become the prerogative of the college girl rather than the swagger swain.

I would suggest that the Victoria and Albert Museum would welcome some of these creations, particularly that of the lady third from the right. It must surely have appeared in the fashion pages of those days. Could it possibly have been consumed by moth? It appears to me as though a bomb would be needed to cause its disintegration.

This is Captain Ernest George Pretyman's wedding reception, given to his tenants on the occasion of his marriage to Lady Beatrice Adine Bridgeman, eldest daughter of the fourth Earl of Bradford. He is fourth from the left in the front row and his lady is on his left.

He was the eldest son of the Reverend Canon Frederick Pretyman, rector of Great Carlton, Lincolnshire and Canon of Lincoln cathedral. He is easily found in the front row, next to his daughter-in-law and the lady with a bosom, was a cousin somewhat removed of the great Colonel Tomline. The Orwell Park Estate, as well as that of Riby in Lincolnshire had been left to him in trust, one of the trustees being his own father.

Ernest George Pretyman, born in 1859, was educated at Eton and the Royal Military Academy, Woolwich. He entered the Royal Artillery, 1880, and retired as Captain, 1889. He was Colonel, 1st Suffolk and Harwich Garrison Artillery Volunteers; he was elected Conservative M.P. for the Chelmsford Division of Essex. He was a J.P. and Deputy Lieutenant for Lincolnshire, becoming Conservative M.P. for S.E. Suffolk, 1895–1906; he was Civil Lord of the Admiralty, 1900–3, and Parliamentary Secretary to the same, 1903–5. He became a Parliamentary Secretary to the Board of Trade, 1915–16, and Civil Lord of the Admiralty, 1916–19. And this is what was said of him at the time:

The adventurous spirit of England finds an outlet either in the army or in politics. Mr Pretyman, the son of the Canon of Lincoln Cathedral has in both given vent to his courage and enterprise. He was a Captain in the Royal Artillery when he was left an inheritance by a relative, and quitting the army he soon entered the House of Commons.

He was not long in the House before he became conspicuous among young members of the Conservative Party below the gangway as much by his attractive exterior and winning address, as by his clear, cogent and sincere style of speaking. Soon he was invested with the responsibilities of office. In the Balfour administration he was first Civil Lord of the Admiralty and then Parliamentary Secretary to the department.

It needs a man of practical common sense, and an indefatigable worker, to deal promptly and sagaciously with the multiplicity of affairs that come up for settlement in the great department of the Admiralty, and by general acknowledgement, Mr Pretyman's soundness and sobriety of judgement was never at fault.

It should be realized that the captain was a very different person from his litigious relation. He did very nice things with his property and became one of the builders of modern Felixstowe, carrying on the work and vision of his predecessor and was most generous in his benefactions. For example he gave the site of St John's Church in Felixstowe. The foundation stone was laid by Lady Pretyman and this was her first public engagement after she was married. The spire, 175 feet high, and a wonderful landmark, was given by him in memory of his father in 1914.

But there is more in the photograph than all that, because the company is so full and, in the main, of local names that meant so much to the neighbourhood at the time. These include many whose descendants still figure in the locality; but some have passed on, because whereas the neighbourhood was then purely agricultural it has now become urbanized largely through the docks of which the old Colonel cut the first sod. They were considerable farmers, such as Clement Smith, Cordy, Hyem, Allen, Last, Posford, Hunt, Hobbes and Dawson.

Some of those names appear in the Suffolk Stud Book, remembering it was a horse-drawn age, and the Suffolk Punch was preeminent amongst Suffolk horses, indeed above all shire horses. Its pedigree was almost a sacred tree, and purity of breeding was only equalled by the Suffolk squirearchy; and Captain Pretyman was one of its devotees.

15

BORN AT DEPDEN

Know most of the rooms of thy native county before thou goest over the threshold thereof.

Thomas Fuller

First as to its location: Depden is about seven miles south-west of Bury St Edmunds in the district of Thingoe, West Suffolk. It shares with the adjoining parish of Rede the highest land (420 feet) in Suffolk, which is part of a plateau extending across the county. The clay lands are in the driest part of England.

Hatherly John Woollard, from whose delightful family record I give extracts by his permission states:

My birthplace (1899) was a small brick-built semi-detached cottage, across the road from Depden Elms Farm. Father, a farm labourer was then thirty-four and mother twenty-seven. Sister Gertrude was born in 1900, and after the birth of my brother Ernest in 1903 the family moved to the Bury district.

To give help to my mother for a short term I was placed with my grandparents and Aunt Ellen (Nellie) at Clay Hall, which was only a short distance from Depden Elms. My grandparents had been at Clay Hall at least since 1861 when uncle Harry was born, having taken over from a Thomas Palmer.

I remained at Clay Hall because assistance to mother was welcome as another baby was born early in 1905. Possibly a baby in the house meant a great deal to the people in the home.

From this time events and influences which have a great part in shaping the life of a person started to operate, and it will be evident throughout this record that events rather than conscious striving have been the key to my progress. I hope and believe I have not been indolent.

Clay Hall, situated on the rather remote east side of Depden, adjoining Rede parish, was not a substantial or imposing building as the name might suggest, but two large semi-detached cottages in the Suffolk style of two to three hundred years ago with over an acre of ground. Our neighbour, Henry Pask, had less than half an acre share but he had been the occupant when the Tithe Roll was compiled in 1839. At the time Kersey Cooper (he was agent to the Duke of Grafton) owned the land together with three other adjoining acres and also Black Wood (midway between Clay Hall and Clopton). . . .

There was no school at Depden, so a journey on foot of two miles each way had to be made for attendance at Chedburgh school, which was no hardship for children who were accustomed to walking whatever the circumstances.

If the village could be said to have a centre I suppose it would be Depden Green — one and a half miles distant — where was a small cottage shop, and a windmill in full sail. Having been inside the mill it was no surprise in later years to hear persons with the name of Miller referred to as Dusty. For the rest of our needs from outsiders we depended to a large extent on travelling traders, except for a coffin. Joe Spurling, a wheelwright, lived at Depden mending and making farm equipment, occasional pieces of domestic furniture and coffins. Looking back to those days it seems quite appropriate that Joe should have been sexton at the church. Much time was spent on my way home from school watching the arrival of the trees, the sawing of planks or the shaping for cart wheels, spokes, hubs and all the other requirements.

As school children we were part of the surroundings of nature without any uncertain diversions. We developed physically and changes and education proceeded as part of normal life. The manner in which boys and girls in the open attended to their needs was little different from what we saw in the fields and farmyards. When a fine Suffolk Punch stallion with a bag of corn attached to a light harness, its mane and tail decorated with highly coloured tape and with a groom walking alongside, passed me on a school journey, I knew the purpose and would remember to watch for the foal at Depden Elms Farm. These strong and heavy horses were necessary for ploughing and other work on the heavy clay soil of Depden.

No public house existed in the village which as far as I was aware was no drawback, since the housewives made their own wines in variety, e.g. sloe gin, parsnip wine, mead and in many families a barrel of beer was available from the home brewing. Home made embrocation and simple medicines were also to hand.

For food we were practically self-sufficient, largely due to the routine of grandfather, who regarded God given daylight as the right measure of activity; up with the birds and to bed soon after sunset. When I recall that my grandparents were around seventy years of age when I was born, I marvel at their strength and ability to raise crops, pigs, poultry, bees for honey and wax, and to keep in order nearly an acre of ground. Potatoes and other root crops had to be planted, and after harvesting stored in clamps, greens grown, corn sown, reaped and thrashed, pigs and poultry fattened, killed, and in the case of pork, salted, and chaps smoked for future use. Aunt Nellie gave a full share of help, but she had a deformity of her left arm and hand.

I have a vivid memory of sitting at the hearth in an area large enough to contain a brick and iron fire basket, two high-back chairs and a bench. Looking up the large chimney I saw pork chaps hanging in the lower part, and at the top opening stars shining. On occasion snow would gently fall to be melted as it reached the fire provided by logs of wood which had been cut and stored.

Adjacent to the fire place in the living room was the oven for baking bread etc., which was a weekly event, when faggots had to be brought in from the back yard for burning to create embers of the right heat before the dough loaves were put inside. Grandmother and Aunt Nellie did this work, apart from garment making, sewing, not only for the household but also piece work to gain a small income from traders who availed themselves of this kind of manufacture. My contribution to the baking routine was to go to the "Queen", a public house on the Ickworth side of Chedburgh and collect a pennyworth of yeast. I must confess to eating some on the way home, and I thought it to be a fair reward for the journey. Greene, King & Sons informed me that the "Queen" was closed around 1920, and is now the residence of Sir

George Mallaby, who has given me some helpful information and suggestions.

Apart from the living room there was also a small bedroom at ground level and a back house (pronounced "bacchus") which was used for work and storage. All the floors downstairs were made of large flat stones and bricks. Upstairs were two bedrooms, access to the smaller one being through the main room. Of course no ceiling in the modern sense existed, the upright timbers of the walls being shaped to form an apex.

It is evident from the marriage certificate that neither grandfather nor grandmother did much if anything in the way of writing, but perhaps that increased their ability to memorize. At any rate I have a vivid recollection of grandfather, in the days of increasing age and inability to go to chapel at Wickhambrook or Chevington, holding his own service seated by a stack of straw. The pages of his bible were dark with use. He knew how to pray and to sing quite lustily. He favoured Sankey and Moody hymns, but why the first line of the chorus 'Pull for the shore sailor, pull for the shore' should have had a special appeal I shall never know, but perhaps the tune was attractive. There was no doubt the sureness of his simple faith, culminated in his last words in March 1911, 'Jesus is coming for me'.

Harvest time was the peak of the year. It was the key to so much for all our lives. Hopes and fears fluctuated according to the weather and the ability to cope. Children knew all this at an early age, and when we joined the women folk in gleaning after the corn had been harvested it was with satisfaction that we added a small mite to the store to be kept to feed the hens etc.

With the ground available at Clay Hall grandfather was able to grow corn. After cutting and stooking it was threshed by hand, the straw to be stacked for thatching and other purposes, and the corn to be taken to Mr Pledger at Depden Green for milling. It was too late in time for me to participate in the harvest horkey. I heard of it from older folk, but I do remember grandfather singing a ditty possibly associated with harvest or Christmas: 'Bring to me the punch and ladle and we will fill up the bowl'.

From what I have already said it is clear that my grandparents were peasants living a very frugal life, and as such they participated in the parish bounty. Depden church had in trust an income from lands in Hargrave and Stansfield, which was distributed about Christmas time. My grandfather received annual payments of five shillings to eight shillings during the years 1866 and 1877, according to the Depden records.

Outings were few and far between, but the rectors (Reverend O. B. Packard until his death in 1908; Reverend A. H. Hamilton who succeeded him) and their families encouraged the village children to attend church, with the highlight of a Christmas party at the Rectory. I remember being Little Jack Horner on one such occasion.

My mother's parents lived at Dodd's Farm, Wickhambrook, about five miles distant, but less by footpath along the fields, and on my way sometimes I would call to see Aunt Annie, my mother's sister who had married Jim Hurst, who lived at Clopton. I was always ready to visit "Granny Dodd". It was when returning from Dodd's Farm with Aunt Nellie to Clay Hall early one night that in the cloudless sky we saw Halley's Comet, and what a memorable experience it was.

To go further afield transport was needed, and that involved arranging a time when we could join the Carrier's cart, which started from Wickhambrook in the morning and reach Bury by midday, after stopping whenever necessary for a variety of reasons. The return journey from the "Three Kings" began about four or five p.m. There was no comfort, as the seat was a wooden plank with little protection against rain, snow or cold. The "Three Kings" is no more, but history cannot be obliterated as today in St Andrew's Street at Bury there is a portion of wall on which those three words still appear, without any meaning for today's generation.

Occasionally a visit to Ickworth Park could be arranged, My cousins Harry and Daisy were living with their grandparents at the White House, Mr Vincent being a gardener employed by the Marquis of Bristol. Uncle Harry had married Maria Vincent at Christmas time, but by a quirk of memory the outstanding feature is a cage in the snow-covered ground for trapping blackbirds, and a meal of blackbird pie.

Looking back, I feel that the seed of my historical sense of Suffolk history was implanted when as a schoolboy I saw Mr Louis N. Parker's pageant at Bury in 1907.

On 20th July 1909 grandmother Woollard died suddenly when sitting in a chair mending clothes. I have no recollection of the event, but as it was a Thursday probably I was at school. But I did join in tending the grave in Depden churchyard.

Now a second event to shape my future was to occur. On an early spring day in 1910 I quenched my thirst by drinking water from a ditch at the side of the road between Depden Elms Farm and Clay Hall, and it was not long before typhoid fever set in. Removal to hospital did not take place, even if it was considered a remote possibility. Instead Dr Wilkin of Wickhambrook was consulted and he told Aunt Nellie what to do, with a strict warning 'no solid food of any kind'. My aunt must have demurred, as the doctor had to add the comment 'You have to be cruel to be kind'.

Excreta had to be buried deep in ground as far as possible from the house in a portion where leakage into water was unlikely, and I was to drink only boiled water with a little brandy. How to get the brandy? The rector Reverend Hamilton, harnessed his pony and trap and solved the problem by travelling to Bury. Subsequent news which reached me spoke of delirium, the fear of people to approach the house, and of a critical stage when Dr Wilkin said, 'I have done all I can. It is now in God's hands.'

After the crisis I well remember a craving for Sneezum's sausages; alas no longer available at the corner of Risbygate Street, Bury. It was not until many years later that I fully appreciated what a strain it must have been for Aunt Nellie.

By June 1910 I had recovered sufficiently for convalescence, and by what means I do not know I had the opportunity to see the sea for the first time at the Convalescent Home, Felixstowe. (Since demolished.) Boy-like, I must have been concerned about the cash available. I took part in the gathering of snails in the grounds at $\frac{1}{4}d$. for twenty, and Aunt Nellie wrote to me on 29th June 1910, 'You will have your sixpence all right'.

We might now leave this record of a Suffolk village lad to state simply a remarkable career. He became a member of the National Bank at Old Broad Street, London, an Anglo-Irish concern, of which Lord Pakenham was appointed chairman in 1955. He became a General Manager in 1959 and on retirement was made a director. He was also made a Freeman of the City of London. Surely a wonderful record under any consideration.

Kelly's Directory for 1879 has this to say about the village:

Depden is pleasantly situated on an extensive green. The church of St Mary is an ancient building of brick and stone, and was completely restored and beautified at the sole cost of the late rector, who expended upwards of £1,500 upon the repairs and stained windows, which are rare and of great beauty: the church consists of chancel, nave, porch and tower with three bells: the service of communion plate is very handsome, the gift of Anthony Sparrow, successively Bishop of Exeter and Norwich, who was a native of Depden: there is a perfect brass in the church to the memory of Lady Ann Jermyn, erected in 1572: the churchyard, which is nearly two acres in extent, is beautifully laid out with small plantations. The registers date from the year 1538. The living is a rectory, yearly value £464, awarded as a rent charge in 1842 in lieu of tithes, with a residence and 24 acres of glebe, in the gift of the Lord Chancellor. The rectory house is a handsome modern building, standing in a pleasant plantation, surrounded by pleasure-grounds. The Marquis of Bristol is lord of the manor and principal landowner. The soil is of rich loam, subsoil clay producing excellent crops of wheat, oats, beans, turnips and green crops generally. The area is 1,595 acres; rateable value £2,157, the population in 1871 was 267. Parish clerk, William Lockwood Manning who was also a sub-postmaster, carrier to Bury George Bennett, Wednesday.

Here follows the principal residents: Woodgate, Reverend James Richard, M.A., J.P.; George Bonnett, baker; James Fisher, farmer; Richard Green, farmer and miller; Robert Green farmer, The Gate; Thomas Green farmer, The Hall; Thomas George Green farmer, Rookery; William Isaacson, farmer; William Isaacson jun. farmer; William Lockwood Manning, blacksmith; George Orbell farmer, The Elms; Isaac Reynolds farmer; Thomas Shave, wheelwright.

From this small community we note there were eight farmers, that William Lockwood Manning held three offices, that Thomas Shave had a most applicable name, that it was a rich living and a tight little community.

A transcript of the Registers in Latin is to be found in the *East Anglian Notes and Queries* for 1891–2. This shows the Sparrow family as first mentioned in 1539 and the last entry in 1683. Likewise the Jermyns are mentioned in 1556 and end in 1641. The Coels appear in 1618 in the person of Sarah, daughter of Thomas Coel baptized in May, and end with Anna Coel buried March 1714–15.

The Hall is merely a site now, and Clay Hall has given place to a modernized building; while the church has been joined up with Rede and Chedburgh, but has remained open under one minister.

16

WITH JOHN EVELYN IN SUFFOLK
(1620—1706)

Where noble Grafton spreads his rich domains,
Round *Euston's* water'd vale, and sloping plains,
Where woods and groves in solemn grandeur rise. . . .
There Giles, untaught and unrepining, stray'd
Through every copse, and grove, and winding glade.

Bloomfield

It is only natural that this remarkable man (Evelyn) should find his way into our county. Considering that his interests were so widely placed, extending from the manufacture of treacle to the increase of witches in New England, it followed as he himself expressed it in one of his letters, that he did not travel merely to count steeples. Besides, in his excursions he made acquaintance not only with men eminent for learning, but with men ingenious in every art and profession. He was a friend and confidant of the Stuart Kings, but did not share in their sometimes wild behaviour. A small part of his epitaph sums him up:

That all is vanity that is not honest
and there is no solid wisdom
but in real Piety.

'1st· August [1672] I was at the marriage of Lord Arlington's only daughter (a sweet child if ever there was any) to the Duke of Grafton, the King's natural son by the Duchess of Cleveland; the Archbishop of Canterbury officiating, the King and all the grandees being present. [The child was then only five years old.] "Worthy for her beauty and virtue of the greatest Prince in Christendom".'

Euston was his chief interest in Suffolk, so near as it is to Newmarket.

First we will join with him as he approaches Ipswich:

> Went to Dedham—hence to Ipswich, doubtless one of the sweetest, most pleasant, well-built towns in England. It has twelve fair churches, many noble houses, especially the Lord Devereux's; a brave quay, and commodious harbour, being about seven miles from the main; an ample market-place. Here was born the great Cardinal Wolsey, who began a palace here, which was not finished.
>
> I had the curiosity to visit some Quakers here in prison; a new fanatic sect of dangerous principles, who show no respect to any man, magistrate or other, and seem a melancholy, proud sort of people, and exceedingly ignorant. One of these was said to have fasted twenty days; but another, endeavouring to do the like, perished on the 10th, when he would have eaten, but could not.

> 1676–77. I went to visit my Lord Crofts, now dying at St Edmunds Bury, and took the opportunity to see the ancient town, and the remains of that famous monastery and abbey. There is little standing entire, save the gatehouse: it has been a vast and magnificent Gothic structure, and of great extent. The gates are wood, but quite plated over with iron. There are also two stately churches, one especially.

And so to Euston.

> A stranger preached at Euston Church and fell into a handsome panegyric on my Lord's [Arlington] new building the Church, which indeed for its elegance and cheerfulness, is one of the prettiest country churches in England. My Lord told me his heart smote him that, after he had bestowed so much on his magnificent palace there, he should see God's House in the ruin it lay in. He has also re-built the parsonage-house, all of stone, very neat and simple.
>
> To divert me my Lord would needs carry me to see Ipswich, when we dined with one Mr Mann by the way. . . . After dinner

came the Bailiff and Magistrates in their formalities with their maccs to compliment my Lord and invite him to the Town-House, where they presented us a collation of dried sweet meats and wine, the bells ringing etc. . . . Then saw the Haven seven miles from Harwich. The tide runs out every day, but the bedding being soft mud it is safe for shipping and a station. The trade of Ipswich is for the most part Newcastle coal, with which they supply London, but it was formerly a cloathing town. There is not any beggar asks alms in the whole town, a thing very extraordinary. . . . We returned late to Euston, having travelled about fifty miles this day.

Since first I was at this place, I found things exceedingly improved. It is seated in a bottom between two graceful swellings, the main house being with four pavillions, two at each corner, and a break in the front, railed and balustraded at the top, where I caused huge jars to be placed full of earth to keep them steady upon their pedestals between the statues, which make as good a show as if they were of stone, and though the building be of brick, and but two stories besides cellars, and garrets covered with blue slates, yet there is room enough for a full court, the offices and out-houses being so ample and well disposed. . . . The chapel is pretty, the porch descending to the gardens. . . .

The canal running under my lady's dressing-room chamber window, is full of carp and fowl, which come and are fed there. The cascade at the end of the canal turns a corn mill, that provides the family, and raises water for the fountains and offices. To pass this canal into the opposite meadows, Sir Samuel Morland has invented a screw-bridge, which being turned with a key, lands you fifty feet distant at the entrance of an ascending walk of trees, a mile in length. . . .

There is a library full of excellent books. There are bathing-rooms, elaboratorie [sic], dispensatorie, a decoy, and places to keep and fat fowl in. He had now in his new church built a dormitory or vault with several repositories to bury his family in. In the expense of this pious structure, the church is most laudable, most of the Houses of God in this country resembling rather stables and thatched cottages than temples in which to serve the Most High. He has built a lodge in the park for the keeper, which is a neat dwelling and might become any gentleman. The same has he done for the parson, little deserving it, for murmuring that my Lord put him some time out of his wretched hovel, whilst it was building. He also has built a fair inn at some distance from his palace, with a bridge of stone over a river near it, and repaired all the tenants houses, so as there is nothing but neatness and accommodation about the estate. . . .

Having now passed here three weeks at Euston to my great satisfaction, with much difficulty he suffered me to look homeward, being very earnest with me to stay longer, and to engage me, would have carried and accompanied me to Lynn Regis, a town of important traffick, about twenty miles beyond, which I had never seen as also the Travelling Sands about ten miles wide of Euston, that have so damaged the country, rolling from place to place, and like the sands in the deserts of Lybia, quite overwhelmed some gentlemen's whole states [The Brecklands]. . . .

My Lord's coach conveyed me to Bury, and thence baiting at Newmarket, stepping in at Audley End to see that house again, I slept at Bishops Stortford, and the next day home.

I began with a quotation from Bloomfield, who returns to his childhood in autumn, when the huntsman's cry was heard:

> Where smiling Euston boasts her good Fitzroy,
> Lord of pure alms, and gifts that wide extend;
> The farmer's patron, and the poor man's friend:
> Whose mansion glitters with the eastern ray,
> Whose elevated temple points the way,
> O'er slopes and lawns, the park's extensive pride,
> Lo! where the victim of the chase reside,
> Ingulf'd in earth, in conscious safety warm,
> Till lo! a plot portends their coming harm.

Evidently they had a famous hound, for a footnote to a following page states that there is an inscription on a stone in Euston park wall: 'Foxes rejoice! here buried lies your foe.'

17

A WEST SUFFOLK MURDER

One murder made a villain,
Million a hero.
Beilby Porteus

An alternative sub-title to the above might be: 'The Murderer
Who Made Crime History'.

Twenty-seven-year-old James Rutterford was the West Suffolk murderer who was the talk of the nation in 1870. He was
the first man ever to be spared hanging because death by
hanging would have been, owing to the structure of his neck,
too cruel to him. He was saved from death by execution. Instead, he went to life imprisonment and died years later in a
London gaol.

The account which follows comes from the *Bury Free Press*
of 8th January 1870, and was republished in their "Century
Story" with this added note. 'Notice the freedom of comment
(unthinkable today) on a case which had not yet come to trial.'

On the last day of 1869, a fearful tragedy was enacted on
the borders of the estate of His Highness the Maharajah
Duleep Singh, in which one of his gamekeepers, a young man
only nineteen years of age, named John Hight, has been
deprived of his life.

It appears from the evidence at the inquest, that the
deceased was out watching on Friday afternoon in a plantation
called "Crinkle Crankle Belt", and two men named James
Rutterford and David Heffer, the former of whom is a
notorious poacher, were seen in the locality with a gun.

The same evening, between six and seven o'clock, Police

Constable Peck was on the look out for poachers, accompanied by an old man, and in walking along the Elveden turnpike road saw "something" moving along about fifty or sixty yards off in a turnip field.

He watched "it" and as "it" came nearer he distinguished that two men were approaching him, one of whom was armed with a double barrelled gun.

On attempting to take the gun away from this man, who it was proved, was Rutterford, he raised it for the purpose of striking the policeman on the head.

The policeman, however, warded off the intended blow, and wrenched the gun away from him. It was afterwards ascertained that both barrels were loaded.

On Saturday night it was rumoured that Hight was missing and a search was instituted and continued till after dark by aid of lanterns, but no trace of him could be found.

On the following (Sunday) morning a party of about thirty men resumed the search, and in a piece of furze encircling the edge of the plantation his mangled body was discovered.

The circumstances aroused the constable's suspicion, and he further examined the gun and found a quantity of blood on the barrels bent in, and from a slight crack where the barrel was bent, he picked some hairs.

This circumstance, in conjunction with Rutterford and Heffer being stopped within a mile of the scene of the murder and within an hour of the supposed time of its occurrence, led to their apprehension and they were taken before a magistrate and remanded.

A more minute search of the plantation on Sunday revealed the fact that the spot where the poor fellow was found was not where he had been attacked and killed, for at a distance of 139 paces the deceased's stick, and a large pool of blood, covered over with leaves, pointed out that as the spot where the struggle, if indeed, any time for a struggle had been allowed the deceased, had taken place.

It is believed that the deceased must have come suddenly

upon his murderers, while they were in the very act of poaching, and that he then and there received his death blow.

From the fact that his body was found in such a distance from the place, it is believed that more than one person was engaged in the affair.

The deceased's seal-skin cap has not been found and it is rather singular the policeman Peck searching Rutterford at the time he took the gun, he felt something in his coat pocket which he described as very soft, and when asked what it was Rutterford replied that it was his old cap.

The very heavy rain on the night of the murder had entirely obliterated all traces of footmarks, so that whether the deceased was dragged or carried to the place where he was found it was impossible to say.

He had certainly been moved by the arms, which were left extended upwards over his head and had so become rigid.

The surgeon also speaks of his waistcoat and neckerchief being pulled over his face, leading to the belief that he had been dragged by his clothing. The evidence of the surgeon who examined the body is fully confirmed by the shocking appearance the head of the deceased presented when viewed by the jury. There are in all seven lacerated wounds on the face and head — three on the lower and four on the upper part.

The deceased, who is a native of Brigstock, Northamptonshire, was much respected in the neighbourhood where he has been for only a few months, and great indignation and horror were manifested when it was seen how brutally he had been injured.

It is exactly nineteen years ago this Christmas that a similar occurrence took place in the same locality.

The Prince Duleep Singh was present at the inquest and took a deep interest in the proceedings.

The prisoners who affected to treat the matter very lightly, have been remanded by the magistrates for a special hearing and the coroner adjourned the inquest till Monday 17th January at eleven o'clock.

Of the two prisoners Rutterford is the older and tallest, and his appearance is not that at first sight very favourable for him, caused by his face having been disfigured by a burn some years ago. Heffer appears to be about twenty-four years of age, with a smooth face, and is one of the ordinary type of farm labourers.

They both up to the time of the inquest protested their innocence, but the police are diligently following up every clue that presents itself, and we earnestly hope that the perpetrators of this dastardly outrage will meet with the punishment they so richly deserve.

It was at the end of March that Rutterford came up for his trial at the Suffolk Assizes at Ipswich. Heffer turned Queen's evidence and left the court a free man.

After a two-day hearing before Mr Justice Byles the prisoner was found guilty and sentenced to death. The *Free Press* issued a special supplement to report the trial. This took up two pages of close print.

A petition was organized for his reprieve. There was much sympathy for him in West Suffolk, and much antipathy to him too.

Mr John Fincham of Beck Row (Mildenhall), wrote as follows at the time:

We are sorry that the local journals have all along described the convicted as a desparate character, which, no doubt, had great weight with the judge and jury.

Rutterford is well known to be of a very kind disposition, assisting any of his neighbours at any time. . . . We have invariably found him a quiet well-conducted young man, and I think I am right in saying that he has never once been before the Bench for assault.

I am very sorry to say that the neighbourhood in which Rutterford and his parents have been brought up, for generation after generation, has never had the least facility for education of any kind.

This and the next hamlet, being between two and three miles

from Mildenhall, the inhabitants could not, with few exceptions, attend a school at Mildenhall.

This dark corner has been much neglected by all religions — at least Holywell Row has — and had it not been for the Dissenting School at Beck Row, which is a Sabbath School, there would not have been the least opportunity afforded for their moral improvement.

We now hope something will shortly be done to improve this hamlet. As to Rutterford, I am at a loss to know how he was capable of committing the foul deed for which he has to suffer, but it appears as if he was for a time beside himself; fear of being punished made him, no doubt, commit that awful deed.

Rutterford was reprieved following a medical report which was placed before the Home Secretary. This is what the report said:

We, the undersigned, John Kilner and Thomas Coe, two qualified medical practitioners, being duly appointed . . . have, together with Dr Macnab, the surgeon to the goal, proceeded to examine James Rutterford . . . and the cicatrix which he has in his neck, and hereby report that in our opinion he cannot be hanged by ordinary means, for to secure against the risk of failure and a prolongation of suffering, it will be necessary to use a very considerable and unusual amount of constricting force before the rope can be adjusted in such a manner as to sustain the weight of the prisoner's body.

The reprieve was greeted by a storm of abuse, but there was a minority in favour of the decision.

18

THE MAHARAJA DULEEP SINGH

If to far India's coast we sail,
Thy eyes are seen in di'monds bright.
Gay

Since Suffolk was intimately connected with H.H., The Maharajah Duleep Singh, it is of interest to give a résumé of the career of this Indian Prince who was proclaimed Maharajah at the age of five, and who was the putative owner of the famous Koh-i-noor diamond. The following record is taken from *Lady Login's Recollections*, edited by her daughter, E. Dalhousie Login, 1917.

Sir John Spencer Login was installed by Henry Lawrence as Governor of the Citadel of Lahore, and also as governor of the young dethroned king, Duleep Singh, a very lovable, intelligent and handsome boy of twelve years old, who very speedily developed a great affection for his guardian. His great amusement then was hawking or falconry. He was unusually well educated for an Indian prince of those days, reading and writing Persian very well, and having made some progress in English.

Amongst the treasures of the Citadel was the Koh-i-noor, always kept under a strong guard. Lord Dalhousie related how Login used to show it on a table covered with black velvet, the diamond alone to be seen through a hole in the cloth. Incidentally, the jewel had had a long history, passing through many hands. It was said that its value was "good fortune"; for whoever held it was victorious over his enemies. It was eventually passed to Lord Dalhousie who gave this receipt:

'I have received this day from Doctor Login into my personal possession, for transmission to England, the Koh-i-noor diamond, in the presence of the members of the Board of Administration, and of Sir Henry Elliott, K.C.B., Secretary to the Government of India.

Lahore, 7th December 1849.   Dalhousie.'

A footnote states:

> The Koh-i-noor sailed from Bombay in H.M.S. *Medea* on 6th April. I could not tell you the time, for strict secrecy was observed, but I brought it from Lahore myself! I undertook the charge of it in a funk, and never was so happy in all my life as when I got it into the Treasury at Bombay. It was sewn and double sewn into a belt secured round my waist, one end through the belt fastened to a chain round my neck. . . . My stars what a relief it was to get rid of it.

Duleep Singh's mother was the beautiful and notorious Maharanee Jinda (or Chunda), sometimes known as the "Messalina of the Punjab".

> Everyone was struck with the young Sikh Soverign's manner; his geniality and love of truth, and his straightforwardness was very unusual in an Oriental. One could not but have great sympathy for the boy, brought up from babyhood to exact the most obsequious servility; and it was greatly to his credit that he submitted at all to any direction or discipline, or the idea that his education was to be enforced by any system of authority. My husband was very fond of him and the two got on famously together.

So wrote Lady Login.

The youthful Maharajah suddenly announced his intention of embracing the Christian religion. Enquiries were made that no undue influences had been at work, as this was a very serious step. He used to persuade a young Brahmin from the American Mission School to read the Bible to him, who put it thus: 'Sometimes Bible, sometimes a few conjuring tricks (of which he was very fond), sometimes games in the *Boys' Own Book*.' But it was not until 8th March 1853 that he was baptized, the water from the Ganges being used.

He was brought to England, the first Indian prince to be so acknowledged by the English Government. He was received at Windsor and Queen Victoria decided that his rank should be that he took prescedence after the royal family. He became a great favourite with the Queen and the Prince Consort. But when her Majesty thought he ought to wear something warm as coming from a hot climate, she received this rather daunting reply:

'Indeed Ma'am, I cannot bear the flannel next to my skin. It makes me long to scratch, and you would not like to see me scratching myself in your presence.'

By the Queen's wish he gave sittings to Winterhalter for a full-length picture (now at Osborne House). He was then about sixteen or seventeen, a very handsome youth.

The Queen at this time made enquiries of Lady Login as to whether he ever mentioned the Koh-i-noor: 'Does he seem to regret it and would he like to see it again?' His answer was: 'Yes, indeed I would!'

The "mountain of light" and symbol of the sovereignty of India had been recut by a Dutch firm and made smaller.

During one of the sittings, when the Prince Consort was talking to the painter, a company of beefeaters from the Tower came in their scarlet uniforms escorting an official bearing a small casket which he handed to Her Majesty, who called out: 'Maharajah, I have something to show you!' and she placed the casket in his hands.

He held it for a quarter of an hour, turning it from side to side, then moving to the Queen he handed it to her with these words: 'It is to me Ma'am, the greatest pleasure thus to have the opportunity as a loyal subject of myself tendering to my Sovereign the Koh-i-noor.'

He was often at Windsor and Osborne, and when at the latter he was delighted at the friendliness of the royal children towards him, especially the young princesses, who invited him with their brothers to the Swiss Cottage in the woods to sample their cooking.

In June 1850 the subject of marriage came into prominence and a native princess was thought to be the person. She was the daughter of the ex-rajah of Goorg, then living in Benares. The Queen took much interest in the little girl, and provided they were to like one another, thought it a good arrangement. But the Maharajah refused the young woman as being unsuitable.

In 1861 Duleep Singh decided to return to India for tiger shooting. He there met with his mother, who for many years had been the virtual prisoner of an unsavoury character of Nepal, Jung Bahadour. They came to Brighton and Lady Login described her first sight of her, in semi-darkness, an aged half-blind woman, sitting huddled on a heap of cushions on the floor.

In 1863 the Logins came to Felixstowe and Lady Login's description of the place is of considerable interest. It was then a small fishing village with one hotel (the "Bath"), and a few lodging houses. 'We had been there only a short time when, on 1st August, a frantic telegram arrived, despatched by mounted messenger from Ipswich, twelve miles off, then the nearest telegraph office, in which the Maharajah implored my husband's presence in London, as his mother had died that morning.' As a result her body was temporarily housed in a vault in Kensal Green Cemetery, until it could be transferred to India for the Hindu funeral rites.

On 1st October 1863 Sir John Login died suddenly at Felixstowe. It appeared that he had returned from India in the spring and had caught a chill through wearing insufficient clothes. Their house was on the sea front, now a part of Felixstowe College, and the funeral to Old Felixstowe Church, a mile away, was a walking one. The Maharajah attended the funeral and walked at the head of the procession with the two sons.

He had just purchased Elveden, hoping to make it a home and a burial place for his family; he did manage to turn it into a semi Indian Palace. It was his intention that the burial at Felixstowe should be only temporary and that the body of his former guardian would be moved there. This did not transpire but at his own expense a typical Victorian memorial of red and grey granite was erected and Queen Victoria chose the text: 'The memory of the just is blessed.' *Proverbs* X,7.

Later he paid visits to Felixstowe, staying at the "Bath" and paying calls on Lady Login. He fully intended to have a good time wild-duck shooting on the Deben, for which he had bought a punt and a punt gun. But he could not endure the officious attention of the hotel keeper, who "Royal 'Ighnessed" him at every sentence, and would never leave him alone for a moment, trotting at his heels like a spaniel.

His thoughts now turned to matrimony. He had intended proposing to a society lady but delaying the action he lost her by a day. On 15th November 1863 he sent Lady Login a note: 'I promise to pay Lady Login £50 (fifty pounds) if I am not married by 1st June 1864, provided my health keeps good.'

He met his wife on his way to India to deal with his mother's body. She was a young lady of semi-Oriental birth at the Mission School at Alexandria, and on his way back they were married. She was only fifteen and described as remarkably nice looking with very fine eyes; and her name was Bamba. Queen Victoria received her. She bore her husband six children and died in 1887, being buried in Elveden churchyard.

In his later years the Maharajah got into difficulty with money and had a violent quarrel with the India Office. He decided to return to India to be re-initiated as a Sikh, became rather mentally deranged and died in Paris in 1893. He was buried at Elveden, where the simple headstones are lined up, so different to the memorial at Felixstowe.

An old friend of mine, the Reverend Tyrrel Green, M.A., well known for his brass rubbings, as a boy remembered seeing the coffin of the Black Prince arrive at the local station.

The Logins lived in Felixstowe for some fifteen years and then Lady Login removed to Kent. She died in 1904 and her body was brought back to Felixstowe to lie beside her husband, having been a widow for forty years. Her memorial is really in the modernized Old Felixstowe Church, because it was she, who with other ladies, got things going to enlarge it. She got the bricks for the transepts from the dismantled battery through the War Office. It remains a fine bit of brickwork in the style of Kentish rag.

19

LINGERING MEMORIES

And Suffolk knows the reason why.
Cecil H. Lay

Amongst my correspondence one morning, actually on my birthday, I received this delightful letter, with permission to publish.

'I too have a strong attachment to dear Suffolk. My grandmother was born in Aspall, near Debenham, and as she shared in my "bringing up" with my mother she had a profound influence on my early life, bless her! She was one of the numerous children of a John Balaam, head horseman to the Chevalier family (Gran pronounced it Sheverleer) and Madam Chevalier as they called her, sounded a forbidding figure. Madam remarked to great grandfather that Florence (grandma) did not curtsey to her as she should, and I think great grandfather inwardly quaked at his mistresse's displeasure, probably fancying he would be turned out of his cottage for the rebellious little daughter's behaviour!

'However, I believe Madam was pacified, because he became farm steward and stayed in his cottage until his death at eighty-one years of age.

'Gran went to a penny school which an old dame held in the room behind her little sweet-shop, and lessons waited while teacher served a customer, with great proddings in the big glass jars of sticky sweets.

'In spite of these commercial interruptions Gran learnt poetry, as well as completely sound arithmetic, perfect grammar and excellent hand writing. So good in fact, that in her sixties she could instruct me in the intricacies of long division, which my London school failed to do, and also spelt perfectly and recited "Lucy Gray":

> (I chanced to see at break of day
> The solitary child)

Her assistance enabled me, I know, to win my place at grammar school. Compare the results of a penny school teaching and the results of our present astronomically expensive educational system! What has gone amiss?

'Scaring crows with a cocoa-tin of stones, working as a farm servant at fourteen years of age for one shilling per week, were her first "situations". On Saturday night she washed her one cotton dress, hung it up in the farm kitchen and on Sunday morning, damp it maybe, it would be donned for her day off and the visit a miles across the fields to the overcrowded cottage that was "home".

'Nearly fifteen years old she made her way to London, in the belief that she would find her young man, Herbie Thatcher, who had already ventured to the Great Wen, but she never did find him in London, and so her hard life as servant girl in late Victorian London commenced. But thereby hangs a score of tales.

'Her shopping list for great-grandma was recited to me — "half a stone of flour, 2 oz tea, four pennyworth of pieces". The pieces being meat for the Sunday meat pudding, shared between a dozen people or more. They kept a pig and grew vegetables needed for the family, increased yearly by sets of twins, many who died in infancy. A piece of bread soaked in milk and sugar was wrapped in linen and thrust in the new infant's mouth, and mother and child were confined to their room for one month, till the old midwife gave her consent for their re-emergence.

'Of course the chores fell heavily on Gran, the eldest girl, and on arriving home from school the poor little creature had to set to and wash piles of baby's napkins, much to her distaste.

'I have a photograph of my great-grandparents, both stately and possessing great dignity in their ten-shilling weekly affluence. Many of the children and grandchildren became teachers and we produced one parson, who unfortunately lost his life in World War II.

'My gran was a capable and intelligent lady, who with even *my* pre-war education would have probably done well. She did things I have never done, cycled pre-1914 to Aspall from North London and in the 1914 black-out often cycled to Cambridge and back to London. Also she obtained better conditions for the women munition workers with whom she worked during 1914–1918. So you see the old Suffolk spirit was strong!

'Gentle and stern with me, I was enveloped in love and good guidance, embellished with a little finer points of living that she had learnt in service with one or two good middle-class families.

'Great-grandfather in the middle 1920s still went out with his gun that hung above the fireplace and shot a rabbit which used to arrive as a soggy blood-stained parcel, held by our postman at arm's length! I suppose it was welcome enough. And a breath of Suffolk in our back-yard, poor little creature! Hanging on a nail in the wall!

'Gran's great childhood's joy was to rise at 4 a.m. and go with her father to Ipswich market with his horse and waggon for Madam Chevalier, I suppose. How she valued being her father's chosen companion on those chilly, dark and exciting journeys. That *was* a great thing in her life and made up for many hardships at home.

'If I was a little fractious she would say — "That owd black dog's on your back again"; and "hodmedod" was the snail we occasionally saw in our polluted garden in London.

'"Harvest Home" was another happy remembered event of her Suffolk childhood, and "elevenses" a bottle of cold tea taken to her father in the field. I saw him when I was four years old (1924) ploughing with Duke and Violet, his beloved horses. I have a photograph of him at that time, in his broad-brimmed hat.

'My dear Gran, born in 1872 died in 1946, in time to see me married and produce her only great-grandchild, my son. A true Christian lady, kind and happy, married to a dour Scotsman, and I believe she was a migraine sufferer she always had bad headaches until she died, but carried on until the end. The Suffolk stoicism!'

The letter then changes and becomes personal:

'My other tie with Suffolk was my school vacations in the early 1930s, not spent with relations, but by sheer chance, in the village of Waldringfield, which is downstream from Woodbridge. A lasting influence, too, on my life! What wonders of nature were discovered here, an interest in archaeology and history, never to leave me, and a permanent memory of the lovely estuary, the dear people, natives and yachtsmen alike, the beautiful heath, now much despoiled, trips to Bawdsey on the *Sea Gypsy*, owned by a fine old Harwich seaman, Captain Wilkinson. The mystery of the trips across the river and the Camelot round the bend that was Woodbridge.

'Ramsholt and Margaret Catchpole, and those dear voices of the old 'uns and the young 'uns of Woodbridge. "Daahris" they called me (Doris) so when I came back to school I was speaking Suffolk, "that was" instead of "it was", and "lil owd boy". No wonder I didn't go down well at school, except with my English teacher in relation to my essays, which at every opportunity were written around the *one* place in my life, Suffolk!

'I was only reading my old essays this week and the magic is still there. I was rather surprised how well I wrote in those days. Prophetically too: Sutton Hoo was not news in 1933, but there I had written a story of the long-boats and strange happenings over the other side of the river, which was not far from the subsequent famous site!

'Lots of helmeted Vikings (actually Saxons they should have been), my only bit of clairvoyance in my life! The theme was their wrath at their tumuli being disturbed; but I had in mind the tumuli on Martlesham Heath, which had awakened my interest in pre-history etc.

'And the beach-combing. I still have sharks' teeth and little fossils picked up in those halcyon days, on the little strand of Waldringfield.

'With great misgivings I visited the dear place last year, but it has scarcely changed, thanks to the rector of the parish, no doubt. Many of my dear friends lie in the churchyard. The church where Easter was primroses and sparrows twittering at the windows, and the Sunday-suited solemnity of Mr Aldous tolling the one bell.

'I bless my dear mother for saving her shillings so that I could have this priceless memory. Poor dear, she had to support herself and me, her daughter, and on £2.10*s*.0*d*. (old money) it was hard going. So she sent me away each school holiday so that I wasn't "kicking about the streets" while she slaved as a book-keeper. She inherited the fierce Suffolk independence, and rather than spend her life with a man she did not love, she left my father, who didn't seem very upset about it all, and gave me a wonderful childhood for a working-class family in the 1920s.

'I think the name Balaam should be spelt Baylham, from the village of that name.' (And so do I.)

20

A SUFFOLK MEMORY

Ere the parting hour go by,
Quick, thy tablets, Memory.
Arnold

Can you remember when you could get a tea for sixpence? I can, so delightful if after a long walk. And if my memory serves me right, you might be lucky enough to have a new-laid egg, one of those nice brown eggs, included in the price. (I was going to say thrown in; but that is not the correct term.) In any case it would have been the most delicious bread and butter and cakes, with a pot of tea.

I was recently rummaging amongst some old papers when I came across this splendid photograph of a baker's shop at Yoxford, taken one happy day in yester year. It evoked many happy memories. Fortunately the house still stands, *sans* the bay window.

First, it shows an old house, once thatched judging by the pitch of the roof, with leaded windows and probably with land attached. Then it got a little too small, so they clapped on a bit at the side, making it L-shaped, thus providing it with a trifle of forecourt, paved with cobbles and duly railed off with a post and chain barrier. When it became a shop I would not know, but I do like that bay window, so redolent of other days and ways, with the shelves that make a display of sweets, four ounces a penny, that had to be prodded out of the glass jars with a skewer.

The sign above reads: "F. B. Fisher, Baker, Confectioner Etc." Now the Fishers had been bakers in Yoxford for many years, because one appears in the 1879 Kelly Directory as "R.

Fisher, baker". Perhaps F. B. was his son. The sign to the left
of the door reads: "Teas Supplied", while the one further left,
obscured by the flag, speaks of ginger beer. That would have
been a local product, made in Yoxford by William Dennison
at his Steam Works and supplied in those lovely little
stoneware bottles of such pleasant shape and colour. Do you
remember them? They were works of art and, in winter, might
have served as Hot water bottles for the children. That old
ginger beer was mighty good stuff and, although it would not
'knock yar down backards', it was amazingly near the border
line, between T.T. and what they sold at the "Three Tuns",
otherwise known as "Owd Tuns". In any case it came out of
the bottle with a sparkle.

This brings us to the hanging sign on the extreme left, an-
nouncing "Refreshments". Let us *hoop* they kept the sign well
oiled, lest it made a horrid scrattin' noise in the wind. Then,
turning to the extreme right, please note that down-pipe with
its nice little rain-water head. There was a counterpart to that,
leading to the water butt in my grandmother's garden. But
there were, of course, sundry plumbers in Yoxford, including
James Fisk, who was also a well-sinker. It was said that his old
pigs could hear when he was coming home, as far distant as
the brick arch over the railway half a mile away.

We now come to the pony cart and patient old Kitty. There
was no need to tie her up as she only went at one pace. It was
no use shugging at the reins and bawling out, 'Git up Kitty,
dew!' because she knew the day was long enough to do the
round. Those nice old contraptions smelt of hoss ile, Stockholm
tar, sweat and leather. On the box cart, for such it is, is a nice
little wicker basket, which if it did not come from anywhere
else, might have come from George Turtel, basket-maker at
Wickham Market; and perhaps the nice little cart came out
from Mr Holmes's yard. At Wickham Market, by the way,
they had a solicitor by the name of James Pringle Barley, who
was secretary to the Wickham Market Association for the
Prosecution of Felons and a Commissioner for taking af-

fidavits in the Supreme Court.

The boy at the back of the cart, with his clean white apron, is loading up ready for the excursion into surrounding villages—Sibton, Peasenhall Badingham. How nice he do smell to be sure. But he could not find customers everywhere because folks used to bake their own bread in the old brick ovens to last a week; and that was wholly good. Moreover, he would have to go to the back doors of the houses for that was where folks lived. Front doors were for weddings and funerals.

As far as my grandfather's home was concerned, a similar pony and cart used to clip-clop along the dusty road from Leiston, passing the Abbey ruins and Theberton thatched church with its round tower. If Yoxford was the garden of Suffolk, Theberton was a runner-up. But I have never tasted better bread than came out from that Leiston oven, delivered by that floury little cart covered over with mealy sacks; the pony waiting patiently at the quiet gate.

As far as our picture is concerned, that leaves us with three people unaccounted for. Mrs Fisher stands at the open door, complete with white apron and her little daughter in front dressed in a white pinafore. Whether the "little owd mite" on the right is another daughter, or just a "nabor's" child who has got into the picture, I would not know. In any case she is not a gnome or sprite as you might imagine, but a "leetle owd mawther", dressed up in clothes that allow for growing.

You may now ask, when was the picture taken? and why the flags? I would hazard a guess that it was at Queen Victoria's Diamond Jubilee in 1897; in a lovely June English summer. When Sir Rafe Blois (Ralph, always the old English Rafe in Suffolk), was at the Hall; when they rang the bells in Yoxford steeple (you could hear them wholly a long way off, such a sweet sound in that quiet air); and Conversation Corner was where the signpost stands by the old elm-shaded churchyard. In those days they sang "Rule Britannia" and meant it, and if Yoxford had not got a band, Middleton had, and was always ready and willing to join in the frolic.

21

SOME SUFFOLK PRINTERS

Then for Printers, good gracious! what hosts have we got,
Engravers, Bookbinders, and I know not what;
But tho' Printers, no dealings with devils have they,
For their Devils to Angels have all given way.
                    "Old Bungay" as sung at the theatre by
                              Mr Fisher, 1816.

The quincentenary of William Caxton setting up his Printing
Press in England (1476) has been fittingly celebrated in Suffolk as well it might. I was highly amused to notice one writer's
description of him as being an amateur. I suppose he was since
he did not become interested in the newly acquired art, which
he had learnt at Cologne, until he was fifty; before that he was
a mercer.

I like the remark made by Robert Copland (1477–1491),
one of his assistants: 'Caxton begynnge with small storyes and
pamphlets and so to others.' What an illimitable vista that
opens out, the end of which like that of the rainbow can never
be reached. Perhaps that was why his first English book was
the *History of Troy.*

It might be mentioned that he printed Chaucer and Sir
Thomas Malory's *Mort d'Arthur*. Chaucer's grand-daughter,
be it noted, became a De-la-Pole of Wingfield and she is
remembered by a bench-end in Fressingfield Church by her
initials A.P. flanked by the cup and wafer.

If south Suffolk was the birthplace of great artists, north
Suffolk seems to have been the home of great learning and its
dissemination by the printing press.

Printing in Bungay must have commenced at a very early period. Mrs Mann in her *Old Bungay* states that towards the end of the nineteenth century there were several printing works in the town, mentioning the names of John Ashby, Morris, Brightly.

The first was a Quaker, antiquarian and botanist. He contributed several letters to the *Gentleman's Magazine*, under the term "Amicus"; was a friend and contemporary of the local historian, Gillingwater, and left several notes and verses relating to Bungay. He died on 24th November, 1828 in the seventy-fifth year of his age.

Richard Morris started a small printing works in 1794, and Charles Brightly, who had been a schoolmaster in Beccles since 1788, gave up his school there and joined Morris at his printing office. It was he who used the old Bridewell or "Chink", as it was called, for copper-plate engraving; and girls were employed to colour the impressions by hand, colour printing not having been invented.

Mrs Mann writes further, 'Among the engravers were Puterell, Wllis, Edwards and others. Brightly was a man of some enterprise and ability, and the author of a pamphlet on stereotyping, published in 1809. In 1808 he became aquainted with John Childs, who was at that time engaged in a grocer's shop in Norwich.'

J. Ewing Ritchie in his *East Anglia*, says that Brightly had suggested to young Childs that he had better come and help him at Bungay than waste his time behind a counter. Fortunately for them both the young man acceeded to the proposal and travelled all over England driving tandem and doing everywhere a roaring trade. Then he married Brightly's daughter, and became a partner in the firm, which was to become known as John and R. Childs, and afterwards Childs and Son.

It should be mentioned that Bungay was a stronghold of nonconformity, and that all these men were extreme radicals, hence the story that follows.

Ritchie, who was the son of an Independent minister at Wrentham, and who knew the printers writes:

Uncle Robert, as I used to hear him called, was little known out of the Bungay circle. He had a nice house, and lived comfortably, marrying after a long courtship, the only one of the Stricklands who was not a writer. Agnes was often a visitor to Bungay, and not a little shocked at the atrocious after-dinner talk of the Bungay Radicals.

'Do you not think', said she, in her somewhat stilted and tragic style of talk, one day, to a literary man who was seated next her, author of a French dictionary which the Childses were printing at the time — 'Do you not think it was a cruel and wicked act to murder the sainted and unfortunate Charles I?'

'Why man,' stuttered the author, while the dinner party was silent, 'I'd have p-p-poisoned him.' The gifted authoress talked no more that day. Naturally, as a lad seeing so much of Bungay, I wished to be a printer, but Mr Childs said there was no use in being a printer without plenty of capital, and so that idea was renounced.

In 1810 Brightly bought the old Workhouse, near the Common, for £255 and converted it into a Printing Office. The firm soon greatly extended its activities and became one of the largest printers and publishers of periodical works in the kingdom. These were then highly popular. The first was among the pioneers of stereotyping. The first hand-printing press was invented by Earl Stanhope in 1800 and one of these machines stood in the composing room at Bungay until the death of Charles Childs in 1876. Edward Matthews, a pupil of Stanhope, was employed as stereotypist and was the head of the department for many years.

The engraver, William Camden Edwards, was born in Monmouthshire in 1777 and went to Bungay to engrave portraits and illustrations for the Bible, *The Pilgrim's Progress* and other works published by Brightly. On the sudden death of the latter at Stamford, on 6th April 1821, he left Bungay, but afterwards returned and continued there until his death in 1855.

Active and fiery in body and soul, John Childs, with the sympathy and advocacy of Joseph Hume and other members of Parliament, and aided also by Lord Brougham, succeeded in procuring the appointment of a Committee of the House of Commons, to inquire into the existing King's Printers' patent for printing the Bible. The principle upon which the patent was originally granted appeared to be correctness, secured only by protection. This proved to be a fallacy, since faults were found, such as: 'Know ye not that all the righteous shall *not* inherit the kingdom of God.' England patents were held by Strahan, Eyre and Spottiswood and the two universities of Oxford and Cambridge. The result was that Bibles were sold to the public at a greatly reduced price.

It was about 1837 that John Childs became notorious because he refused to pay the Church Rate and was the first person to go to prison for the offence, the sum being 17s.6d. He was proceeded against in the Ecclesiastical Courts, and as he refused to pay solely on religious grounds, he did not contest the matter. He was sent to Ipswich goal and the animous nature of the authorities was shown by the endorsement: 'Take no bail.'

One entire sitting of the House of Commons was devoted to the Bungay Martyr, as Sir Robert Peel termed him.

When in due time he was released, the event was celebrated at Bungay in great style. It was said: 'This day was a great day for Bungay.' There were about six or seven thousand people to welcome his return, and the request of the police that the greatest order might be observed was fully acted up to. He was presented with a piece of plate as a memento. It bore the inscription: 'Presented to Mr John Childs by the friends of Civil and Religious Freedom resident in Bungay and its vicinity, as a testimony of their approbation of his conduct, in passively resisting the payment of Church Rates in the year 1835, for which he was imprisoned eleven days in Ipswich gaol, 7th April 1836.

Robert Childs, brother to John, also gave evidence before

the select committee of 1831. He committed suicide on 29th December 1837 by throwing himself out of an upper window of his house at Bungay.

On 28th May of that year, Daniel O'Connell visited Bungay, where he was the guest of 'the spoiled Child'. At five o'clock a dinner was served at the Theatre, when two hundred sat down to the meal.

A Burlesque on this was sent anonymously to Mr Scott by the *Ipswich Star*, 18th June 1835:

Theatre Radical, Bungay
By particular desire
On Friday, 10th June 1835 will be presented the Comedy
(not Shakespeare's)
of
Much Ado About Nothing

The principal characters by the renowned
John the Martyr
late from Ipswich
In Act I

s A GRAND BANQUET D

n   e
o   Bill of Fare   a
c   c
a   *First Course*   o
e   A Boiled Archbishop   n
D   s

Stewed Curate

A Roasted Rector   A Roasted Rector
A Fricasséed Vicar

Choristers patties   Chorister patties
Deacons Parish Clerks Potted *Deacons*
A Boiled Bishop

Pew Openers   *Remove*   *Pew Openers*
A Roasted Dean
Fried Churchwardens   Fried Churchwardens

A Grilled Archdeacon

Stewed Sexton   Stewed Sexton

Pew Openers   Haricot of Tithing Men   *Pew Openers*
                 A Roasted Lay Impropriator

The Dessert will comprise Iced Ballot, Republican Pippins, O'Connell Jam, Humes Universal Sauce and other delicacies.

The Manager requests the indulgence of the audience to the principal parts of the Performers, who are from an "Independent Company" and have never exhibited in a playhouse.

John Childs died at his house in Broad Street on 12th August 1853, in his seventieth year, and was buried in the vault of the Congregational Church, Bungay. Ritchie said he was emphatically a self-made man and one who had large acquaintances with the reformers of his day. By another account, he was a man of great energy, but obstinate and prejudiced and with forbidding manners.

He was succeeded by his son Charles who was a first rate business man, quite resolute, well educated and always striving after excellence, a strong liberal in politics and a great hater of religious shams.

In June 1832 at the Reform Festival, the Town Pump at Bungay was the centre of interest. A stage was erected over it on which was placed a small printing press, the first ever used in Bungay, with a notice stating it was set up by the late Charles Brightly and J. R. & C. Childs.

A sample of the work done by the firm is not without interest.

A COPY OF CHRISTMAS VERSES
Presented to the Inhabitants of Bungay
by their humble servants
The late Watchmen, John Pye and John Tye

Your pardon, Gentles, while we thus improve
In strains not less *awakening* than of yore
Those smiles we deem our best reward to catch
And for the which we've long been on the *Watch*:

Well pleased if we that recompense obtain,
Which we have ta'en so many steps to obtain,
Think of the perils of our *calling past*,
The chilling coldness of the midnight blast,
The beating rain, the swiftly driving snow,
The various ills that we must undergo,
Who roam, the glow-worms of the human *race*,
The living Jack-o'-lanthorns of the place.

Tis said by some, perchance to mock our toil,
That we are prone 'to waste the midnight oil'
And that, a task thus idle to pursue,
Would be an idle *waste of money* too
How hard, that we the dark designs should rue
Of those who'd fain make light of all we do
But such the fate which oft doth merit greet,
And which now fairly drives us off our beat
Thus it appears from this our dismal plight,
That some love *darkness* rather than the *light*.

Henceforth let riot and disorder reign,
With all the ills that follow in their train;
Let Toms and Jerrys unmolested brawl,
(No *Charlies* have they now to floor withal),
And 'rogues and vagabonds' infest the Town,
For cheaper 'tis to save than crack a crown.

To brighter scenes we now direct your view —
And first, fair Ladies let us turn to you.
May each NEW YEAR new joys, new pleasures bring,
And life for you be one delightful spring
No summer's sun annoy with feverish rays,
No winter chill the evening of your days.

To you kind Sirs, we next our tribute pay:
May smiles and sunshine greet you on your way
If married, calm and peaceful be your lives;
If single, may you forthwith get you wives
Thus whether Male or Female, Old or Young,
Or Wed or Single, be this burden sung:
Long may you live to hear, and we to call
A Happy Christmas and New Year to all.

J & R. Childs, Printers, Bungay.

It appears that John Pye and John Tye were the last of the Bungay Charlies, as they were then called. In addition to his duties as a nightwatchman, John Pye was a printer's pressman for fifty years at the John Childs printing office.

Charles Childs died suddenly on 26th December 1876 and the business was sold to Messrs Clay, Son & Taylor of Bread Street, London, and became known as the Chaucer Press; great numbers of antiquarian books, early English texts, and other works being printed there.

Of the young men coming under the influence of the Childs one of the most successful was Bernard Bolingbroke Woodward, librarian to Queen Victoria. He started life as a bank clerk in Norwich for two years, from which he passed to Highbury College and took his B.A. at London University. He became Independent minister at Wortwell, near Harleston in Norfolk, but owing to continual dissensions he resigned, and coming in contact with the Childs he became a reader and corrector of the press in their printing office. He edited for the firm a new edition of *Barclay's Universal English Directory*.

In 1860 on the death of a Mr Glover, who had filled the part of librarian at Windsor Castle for many years, Woodward's name was mentioned to the Prince Consort, in reply to inquiries for a competent successor. Acting on the advice of a friend at headquarters, Woodward forwarded to Prince Albert the printed testimonials he had sent to a large society when he had applied for a secretarial post. These were sufficient and he was appointed.

An interview took place at Windsor which was highly satisfactory; but before the appointment was made Woodward pointed out there was one circumstance that he had omitted to mention and which might disqualify him.

'Pray, what is that disqualification?' asked the Prince.

'It is', replied Woodward, 'that I have been educated for, and have actually conducted the services of an Independent congregation in the country.'

'And why should that be thought to disqualify you?' asked

the Prince. 'It does nothing of the sort. If that is all, we are quite satisfied and feel perfectly safe in having you for a librarian." Woodward began the re-arrangement of the fine collection of drawings by the old masters at Windsor.

He married as his second wife Emma, seventh daughter of George Barham (my mother's maiden name) of Withersdale Hall, Suffolk. He died at his official residence, Royal Mews, Pimlico, on 12th October 1869.

It might be mentioned that a Thomas Miller opened a business as a bookseller at Bungay. He published a catalogue of his books, which were of such variety as to be almost unique. In 1795 he circulated a token, which is known to collectors as the "Miller halfpenny". It bears a likeness of Miller on one side and on the reverse, "Books" and "1755", above which is a beehive radiated. It is now rare and valuable. In 1802 he moved to Albemarle Street, where he became one of the most famous publishers in London, and was succeeded by John Murray.

Richard Clay, the Chaucer Press, are still in the forefront of the printing world, with their much larger neighbour of William Clowes & Son, Ltd at Beccles.

David Stanford in an article on printing in the centenary supplement of the *East Anglian Daily Times*, 1974, states that a press was established in Ipswich before 1556. He goes on to tell of the revolution in the printing industry caused by the introduction of power-driven machines and mechanical typesetters. He lists the important factors of the abolition of the advertisement tax in 1853, of newspaper stamp duty in 1855, and of paper duty in 1861. He goes on to remark the change from the traditional family-owned business to the limited liability concern and that printers often also fulfilled the role of stationer, through the combination of printer and bookbinder. 'However, a very important part of the industry, then as now, was the small printer, the real Master Printer, a man who combined the talents of typesetter, pressman, finisher, administration and financial controller.'

Apprentices were indentured for seven years and printing still had the image of a craft rather than an industry. Printers have been always a gregarious people, not forgetting their wazygoose, or works outing. Among the companies considered to be leaders in the field for quality and technical excellence are Cowell's of Ipswich, who are renowned all over the world for their fine colour printing.

One of the noted publications of the *East Anglian Daily Times* was the *East Anglian Miscellany*. This commenced in 1901, when Charles Partridge undertook the editorship upon 'Matters of History, Genealogy, Archaeology, Folk-lore, Literature' etc. He was followed by the Reverend Edmund Farrar, and he was succeeded in 1935 by Mr Harold Lingwood, until it ceased in 1958. In a record of fifty-six years of publication, a great store of material was gathered together which is of inestimable value to those researching into the history of East Anglia.

A SUFFOLK PARSON AND NEW ZEALAND

Every reform was once a private opinion, and when it shall be a private opinion again it will solve the problem of the age.

Emerson

Edward Gibbon Wakefield (1796–1862), the great colonial reformer, was very closely connected with Suffolk. First through his cousin, John Head, a Quaker who lived at Ipswich, and later by his sister, Cathrine Gurney Wakefield who married the Reverend Charles Martin Torlesse in 1823, who became vicar of Stoke-by-Nayland, one of Suffolk's most beautiful churches, in 1832 and held it until 1881. Catherine was a very beautiful girl with large brown eyes. Wakefield's father and mother were the subjects of a Gainsborough painting. Indeed Wakefield was of Quaker origin and a cousin of Elizabeth Fry.

It might be mentioned that Wakefield, a very impetuous young man, spent three years in Newgate for abducting a young girl for his second wife, having lost his first in childbirth. This so-called marriage was annulled and he never married again. His first step on his release was to take a house in London, and it was to his sister's home in Stoke that he paid frequent visits, usually renting a little cottage there, so that he might take his beloved dogs with him.

It was during these visits that he became deeply impressed by the sterling qualities and the hopeless, down-trodden condition of the Suffolk labourers. It was the era of "Captain

Swing" and the rick-burnings after harvest; as also that of transportation. It was to relieve this poverty that inspired Wakefield to his life's work.

The Act under which South Australia was finally constituted in 1834, embodied all Wakefield's leading principles: the sale of land at a fixed price, not less than 12s. an acre, the employment of the money derived from land sales as an emigration fund, thus providing labour for employment, for the complete and permanent exclusion of convicts. And lastly for the establishment of self-government as soon as the population reached 50,000. He was described as the real 'father and founder' of South Australia.

New Zealand was his chief sphere of work, where a company was formed very much on the lines of that for South Australia which received a Charter in 1841. The Torlesse family was keenly interested, especially when their childrens' old nurse, Naomi and her husband, William Songer decided to go as colonists; and Arthur, Wakefield's brother offered to take his young nephew, Charles Torlesse as a surveyor.

Both Catherine Torlesse and her husband had always warmly sympathized with Wakefield's colonization schemes and had done everything they could to promote emigration from Stoke. They lived too close to the hearts of the poor in the neighbourhood not to realize the immense advantages of the greater opportunities in a new land, to those in the old country which were negligible. And it was as a result of their activities that quite a large number of Stoke families emigrated to New Zealand. (However, it certainly looks a prosperous village by the 1879 directory, when Walter William Winney was the shoemaker and kept the post office.)

Miss Frances Torlesse wrote a small volume *Bygone Days* in which she describes these activities. Many of the farmers objected although others appreciated the motives. She recalls how piles of clothing used to be made regularly for the families. How every year a box filled with all kinds of useful household articles was sent, and how she as a small child regarded it as her part to collect acorns, beech nuts, chestnuts and other seeds for the box to be planted in the new land.

Wakefield tried very hard to get his brother-in-law and his wife to emigrate. Torlesse was willing and so was Catherine, but their departure was frustrated by the reluctance of his fellow clergy to part with him. However, Torlesse became a member of the Canterbury Association and assisted in the formation of a Suffolk branch.

One homely touch comes out from Wakefield's visits to Stoke. He became very partial to a toffee made by the owner of a little general shop, that was known as "suckers" to the Torlesse children. He used to take home a store and hand it round at his meetings. He said it enabled him to get his motions passed, because it stopped up the mouths of his members while they were struggling to speak. I wonder if it was made by a Miss Ann Pittock, described as a confectioner in the directory?

It is good to know that the very trees that abound in Canterbury Park and gardens in New Zealand, are the trees of old England and Suffolk in particular, sent out as seeds by the daughter of a Suffolk parson over a century ago.

Envoi

The following note appeared in the *Daily Telegraph* for 2nd July 1977:

> Seeds more than 2,000 years old, found preserved in peat during an archaeological dig at a Bronze Age site at West Row Fenn, Mildenhall, Suffolk, are being sent to the University of East Anglia for examination.

Yes, Old Suffolk has come a long way. I wonder if those ancient farmers grumbled at the weather, or were more than satisfied with their crops? Evidently they were careful to put a little bit away for tomorrow, as good old Suffolkers were wont.

INDEX